Reading and Interpreting the Works of

ERNEST HEMINGWAY

Enslow Publishing
101 W. 23rd Street
Suite 240
New York, NY 10011
USA
enslow.com

Lit Crit
Guides

Reading and Interpreting the Works of

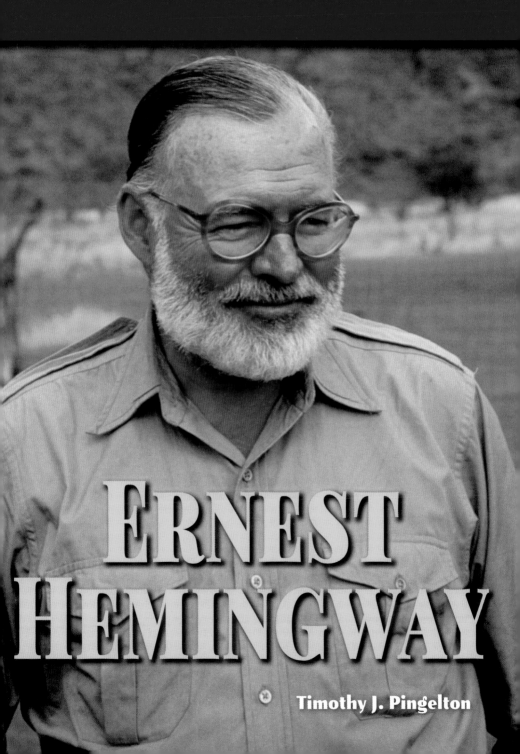

ERNEST HEMINGWAY

Timothy J. Pingelton

Published in 2018 by Enslow Publishing, LLC
101 W. 23rd Street, Suite 240, New York, NY 10011

Cataloging-in-Publication Data
Names: Pingelton, Timothy J.
Title: Reading and interpreting the works of Ernest Hemingway / Timothy J.
Pingelton.
Description: New York : Enslow Publishing, 2018 | Series: Lit crit guides | Includes bibliographical
references and index. | Audience: Grades 7-12.
Identifiers: ISBN 9780766084896 (library bound)
Subjects: LCSH: Hemingway, Ernest, 1899-1961--Criticism and interpretation. | Hemingway, Ernest,
1899-1961.
Classification: LCC PS3515.E37 Z75415 2018 | DDC 813/.52--dc23

Printed in China

10 9 8 7 6 5 4 3 2 1

To Our Readers: We have done our best to make sure all website addresses in this book were active
and appropriate when we went to press. However, the author and the publisher have no control over
and assume no liability for the material available on those websites or on any websites they may link
to. Any comments or suggestions can be sent by email to customerservice@enslow.com.

CONTENTS

Chapter 1   "The Dignity of Movement of an Iceberg":
The Times and Places of Ernest Hemingway ... 7

Chapter 2   From Oak Park to Paris and Beyond:
The Making of the Writer 24

Chapter 3   The Modern Short Story
Collection: *In Our Time* 39

Chapter 4   The Great Cycle of Life: *The Sun Also
Rises*: Bumming Around Europe 55

Chapter 5   Love and Guns: "Francis
Macomber" and *A Farewell to Arms* 68

Chapter 6   "I Went Out Too Far":
The Old Man and the Sea 88

Chapter 7   The Sun Sets: Life Takes Its Toll............. 100

Chapter 8   The Hemingway Legacy: Ernest
Hemingway and His Work Today........... 106

Chronology 115

Chapter Notes....................................... 117

Literary Terms...................................... 121

Major Works by Ernest Hemingway.................. 123

Further Reading 124

Websites.. 125

Index... 126

Ernest Hemingway

"THE DIGNITY OF MOVEMENT OF AN ICEBERG": THE TIMES AND PLACES OF ERNEST HEMINGWAY

Ernest Hemingway and his writing could both be described as an iceberg. Icebergs are strong but can also be fragile; they can drift apart but often group together, and most of their size is hidden. In *Death in the Afternoon*, a book he wrote in 1932, Hemingway wrote about what makes great fiction (prose) writing:

> If a writer of prose knows enough of what he is writing about he may omit things that he knows and the reader, if the writer is writing truly enough, will have a feeling of those things as strongly as though the writer had stated them. The dignity of movement of an ice-berg is due to only one-eighth of it being above water. A writer who omits things because he does not know them only makes hollow places in his writing.[1]

There are many things about Hemingway's life that he did not discuss. There are many places in his writing where detail is left out. The author was not very open to granting interviews, and, in many of his stories, the reader can only guess what the characters look like or even what is really going on. Often, details of the scenes and backgrounds of the characters are left out. In his mind, Hemingway knew what the characters looked like, and, because he was a great writer, the reader is able to picture those characters. With just a few words, Ernest Hemingway was able to paint a detailed image with deep meaning.

Hemingway uses his iceberg theory in all of his writing. The top of the iceberg is what we see on the page, what he shows us. What are the possibilities below the surface? It is fun to consider the possibilities in Hemingway's writing using the iceberg principle.

Read Hemingway like an investigator or detective, thinking about each word (clue) and creating theories. Look at the two opening sentences of Hemingway's 1933 short story "A Clean, Well-Lighted Place":

> It was very late and everyone had left the café except an old man who sat in the shadow the leaves of the tree made against the electric light. In the day time the street was dusty, but at night the dew settled the dust and the old man liked to sit late because he was deaf and now at night it was quiet and he felt the difference.[2]

The old man is sitting in the shadows of a tree, but the shadows are made by an electric light, not the sun. Also, there is no one else at the café. This might be evidence that the old man lives a life unlike most people. Maybe he's pretending he's sitting in the daylight, but he really can't do that for some reason or another. Also, the old man is deaf, but we learn that he can *feel* the difference between the dusty, noisy day and the dewy, quiet night. He prefers the quiet night. This means he is sensitive. Maybe he has good memories of days at cafés, but now he can only go to cafés at night and think of those old times. We wonder what happened to make that change.

The ideas in Hemingway's writing were not entirely new, but the way he wrote was new. In many ways, the writing and life of Ernest Hemingway is like a bridge that connects such concepts as Old World and New World, Victorian and modern, romanticism and realism, traditional and cutting-edge, war and peace, profane and sacred, country and city, life and death.

Born in the Victorian Era

Ernest Hemingway was born at the end of the Victorian era. This period in history ended in 1901, when British Queen Victoria died. It was a time of great literature by the likes of Charles Dickens, Emily Brontë, and Lord Tennyson. Roughly speaking, these writers produced works about how the individual person acts in society, how old ideas can survive with new science, and the failure of traditional ways of looking at things.

For Hemingway, the Victorian attitudes of his parents included such notions as a true man being morally upright and Christian, and women's roles as wives who support their husbands and children. When Hemingway went to Italy to serve in the war effort, his mother feared he would get into trouble and forget to go to church. Hemingway wrote many letters home to her, assuring her that he was being good and that, although he didn't attend church services much then, he was still a Christian.

Hemingway's writing carries much of the Victorian style, but his works bridge modernism and beyond. Modernism broke from old ways of thinking and writing in order to explore new forms, like fiction with endings that are not clear-cut or characters with both good and bad traits. Literature of this period strove to capture life as it really is, without the happy

Queen Victoria was the ruling matriarch who saw the novel format overtake poetry in popularity and realism overtake romantic literature.

endings or unreal characters popular in earlier periods. This kind of writing shocked some people and appealed to others.

A similar change occurred in the visual arts, too. Think of landscape paintings by Thomas Cole or the realist works of Andrew Wyeth. In these, the viewer can easily tell what is being depicted. Now think of impressionistic paintings by artists like Paul Cézanne or Juan Gris. Images in these artists' work don't appear exactly as they do in life because the artists were trying to capture *impressions*: sunlight on a woman's dress can give the viewer the impression of being in the south of France in the spring, near the ocean, feeling a few moments of youthfulness but knowing that old age is near. The surface image is less important than the meaning below it.

Raised in Modernism

In literature, modernism was a movement in which writers broke from the style of the past to explore new ways of writing. The movement is a little different in Europe and America, but it could be said to span from 1900 to 1960. There are different types of modernism. In general, the focus is on common people in common situations. These characters usually have some kind of flaw. They are usually from somewhere other than the setting of the book or story, and they are not sure what they can believe in. Things that once seemed certain to these characters are now uncertain.

modernism
An era when writers wanted to break from the style of the past to explore new ways of writing.

In his writing, Ernest Hemingway uses ideas from the Bible, from Shakespeare, from high-life and low-life people he met, and from other writers and artists. He remembered people and events and used them later in his poetry, stories, and novels. Some things he wrote seem better than they were, and some things he wrote seem worse than they were.

The Shift from Romance to Realism

Hemingway also bridged romanticism and realism. Romantic writers were inspired by medieval stories of brave knights (such as the stories of King Arthur) as well as newer stories in which the hero saves the damsel in distress. In short, romantic literature is fiction in which life is made to seem perfect and the ending is usually happy. Common life is not the focus of these stories, and things turn out just as they should. Passion and imagination are emphasized over realism. There will be a small problem, but the hero will solve it. The popularity of this kind of writing faded toward the end of the 1800's.

As more and more people in Europe and America moved to cities and worked in large factories toward the end of the nineteenth century, literature about far-off, perfect places became less popular. Realism became more interesting to readers. Realism is writing that observes without emotion or without making things perfect, emphasizing people and situations that are more true to life.

Romanticism and realism are seen in paintings, too. A romantic portrait might show someone with flawless skin and wearing nice clothing lying on perfect grass. A realistic portrait might reveal some wrinkles around the mouth of the person wearing clothes that show wear on the elbows, lying on grass that has

romanticism

A movement in writing that emphasizes passion and imagination over realism.

realism

A trend in writing that emphasizes people and situations that are true to everyday life.

some dead patches with rocks showing through. They can both be beautiful portraits, but they are painted in different styles.

A romantic writer might write that a tree is perfectly symmetrical and has shining red apples. The realist writer would describe the flaws as well as the beautiful parts. Things don't always turn out as we think they should, but life is still good. Most writing these days falls in the category of realism.

Here is an example of Hemingway's realism from the beginning of his story "In Another Country":

> It was cold in the fall in Milan and the dark came very early. Then the electric lights came on, and it was pleasant along the streets looking in the windows. There was much game hanging outside the shops, and the snow powdered in the fur of the foxes and the wind blew their tails. The deer hung stiff and heavy and empty, and small birds blew in the wind and the wind turned their feathers. It was a cold fall and the wind came down from the mountain.[3]

This description is very factual and direct. He describes the animals hanging outside the shops in Milan, Italy, without using very many adjectives. The foxes' tails are not described as bushy or soft. We know it is cold, but Hemingway does not use words like "freezing cold" or "bitterly cold" to describe the coldness. This kind of detail is left to the reader to imagine. This realism and factual (or "objective") style is seen throughout nearly all of Hemingway's writing.

Shaping Hemingway

Hemingway was a big reader. It seems he was always reading a book when he had free time. When he was in high school, young Ernest wrote for the school newspaper. He tried to write in the style of Ring Lardner, who wrote humorous short stories, often about sports. He also admired the work of Joseph Conrad, author of the novella *Heart of Darkness*. By reading so much, Hemingway learned the difference between good and bad writing. He also learned how to write without sounding fake.

Ernest Hemingway was also influenced by the visual arts. He appreciated the paintings of Joan Miró, Pablo Picasso, and Paul Cézanne. He thought these painters were better artists than those who painted things just as they look. The painters he liked painted how things *feel*. These painters used color and light to show more than a person can see. They gave their subjects emotion. The way clouds are painted can show emotion, even though clouds can't have emotions. After he left home, Hemingway wrote to his friend Gertrude Stein. He wrote that he was trying to write as Cézanne painted.

"Une Génération Perdue"

In his novel *A Moveable Feast*, published three years after his death, Ernest Hemingway tells the story of how he and his peers acquired the name the "Lost Generation." Hemingway often visited American writer Gertrude Stein in the early 1920s when they were living in separate parts of Paris. He went to Stein's apartment for writing advice and discussion about art. In her apartment, she had several original paintings by artists such as Cézanne, and she knew many famous people. Once he accompanied Stein to get her car repaired. The mechanic was very slow in getting the Model A repaired, and his boss scolded him. Stein overheard the mechanic's boss and used what the boss said to the mechanic to describe Hemingway.

"That's what you are. That's what you all are," Stein said. "All of you young people who served in the war. You are

Gertrude Stein, Hemingway's mentor in Paris, who said people of Hemingway's age were *une génération perdue* ("a lost generation").

une génération perdue [French for "a lost generation"]."[4] Hemingway thought that was a very interesting idea and he used it in his novel *The Sun Also Rises*.

Although Ernest Hemingway did not eagerly embrace the term himself, the name Lost Generation has come to signify a group of American writers whose writing career began in the decade or two following World War I. These writers (F. Scott Fitzgerald, e. e. cummings, John Dos Passos, Hart Crane, and others) found the world after the terrible war to be without justice or faith. The previous generation's values were lost in this new cold, unpredictable, and unfeeling world. Values inherited from their parents and grandparents remained, but the Lost Generation had to change the values to fit the new world. Advances in science, technology, warfare, and the development of a global rather than solely American outlook made the era between World War I and World War II a time of testing values and changing what did not seem to work.

For example, many in the Lost Generation believed that a person could be religious without always going to church. Hemingway's character Nick Adams uses the rituals of setting up camp and fishing on the river in the same way some people use the rituals of a church service. In addition, many in the Lost Generation thought one person exploring his or her beliefs was more important than following the beliefs of a group. A large number of American writers who fought in the Spanish Civil War (1936–1939) fought not for the needs of a country but because they personally wanted fascism to be stopped. Fascism is a political movement in which the nation is more important than the individual, and there is usually a severe leader who silences anyone who speaks against the government. Usually a fascist government has a powerful leader who forces people to do what he wants them to do rather than what is actually good for them. In fascism, people are not allowed to speak out against the government.

Many of these American writers left America and came to Europe (mainly Paris) to enjoy a society that, to them, seemed more worldly, cultured, and relaxed. Very few of these expatriates gave up US citizenship, but they all felt a kind of betrayal by the country many of them had fought for in World War I. Also, it was easier for writers and other artists to live as artists in Paris because the money exchange rate was very favorable to Americans. This lifestyle typically included lingering over long meals at sidewalk cafés, drinking alcohol, and traveling. In the 1920s and 1930s, America was going through very bad economic times, and Paris was more easygoing. For Hemingway, this period in Paris inspired his work as a poet, short-story writer, and novelist.

Clues in the Writing

Ernest Hemingway wrote about what he knew. He served (to some extent) in three major wars, and he wrote about war. He was married four times, and he wrote about love. He attended numerous bullfights, and he wrote about bullfighting. He was an outdoorsman, and he wrote about the outdoors. Although Nick Adams, the character who appears in many of Hemingway's short stories, has many of the same experiences Hemingway had in real life, Hemingway does not let the reader know about the pasts of his characters directly. We have to read carefully and figure these things out like a detective. For example, rather than say that Nick Adams was in the war before coming to fish in the story "Big Two-Hearted River," Hemingway has him set up camp, prepare a meal, and think in such a way as to let the clever reader learn that he was in the war.

Hemingway believed that a good writer could express deep ideas without ruining the mood of a story by having the writer directly tell the reader what to think. The clever writer can show the emotion of a situation by detailing what a character does or how he or she interacts with other characters. If a character's hand is shaking badly after trying to land a fish, and the character sits down heavily afterwards, that might mean that the character has been through some tough times. Nick Adams is healthy, but a tense moment of fishing was too much for him, so he sits to calm down. Maybe he went to the BigTwo-Hearted River to find some peace after some serious event, such as being in a war.

Although much of Hemingway's writing is alive with action, some stories or sections of novels appear to be nothing more than description of a common event or action. In these sections, Hemingway is attempting to create, in as few words as possible, a certain emotion in the reader. After being involved in an interesting experience, his mentor Gertrude Stein advised him, "Find what gave you the emotion; what the action was that gave you the excitement. Then write it down making it clear so the reader will see it too and have the same feeling that you had."[5] Telling readers something specific is difficult, but making readers *feel* a certain emotion can only be accomplished by the very best writers.

Give Them Irony and Pity

In *The Sun Also Rises*, the novel that established Ernest Hemingway as a serious writer, two characters are joking around over breakfast. Bill starts singing a silly song:

> As I went down-stairs I heard Bill singing, "Irony and Pity. When you're feeling . . . Oh, Give them Irony and Give them Pity. [...]"

Hemingway at his typewriter. He started with one true sentence and finished for the day when the action in the story was flowing.

"What's all this irony and pity?"

"What? Don't you know about Irony and Pity?"

"No. Who got it up?"

"Everybody. They're mad about it in New York."[6]

Here, Hemingway is making fun of people who think any novel with irony and pity is a good novel. Irony is a very old writing device. When the speaker means the opposite of what he or she says, the speaker is being ironic. Also, when what actually happens is different from what is expected, that is ironic. Writers of the Lost Generation wrote about scenes with irony because they believed that what is expected may or may not happen. It cannot be controlled. These writers, however, did not treat irony as a joke, as Bill does in *The Sun Also Rises*.

> **irony**
>
> The use of words to express an idea that is opposite that of the words' literal meaning, or when the actual outcome of events is the opposite of what was expected.

Pity is the feeling of sadness or compassion for someone in trouble. Many writers of Hemingway's generation felt pity for the Spanish people who were forced out of their homes by fascists. Once again, pity was a serious feeling; it was not something a writer could just add to a book to make it better. Bill (and Hemingway) is poking fun at writers who use irony to surprise readers and pity to bring emotion into their writing.

There may be much irony and pity in Hemingway's writing, but it is not used merely to sell more books. Irony and pity arise from Hemingway's writing because he felt he was writing about the truth. Hemingway was not satisfied merely to tell his readers about events; he wanted readers to visualize the events and feel the emotions of the characters.

Old Words Are Dead

Another facet of the Lost Generation was their dislike for clichés and overblown, flowery language. They avoided any word that had lost its true meaning. For example, can a writer really define "love" for all readers? "Love" can mean many different things. He believed when words were used without thinking about their true meaning, the words became useless. Hemingway wrote, "Abstract words such as glory, honor, courage, or hallow were obscene beside the concrete names of villages, the numbers of roads, the names of rivers, the numbers of regiments and the dates."[7]

Rather than telling what love is in limited words, he demonstrated what love is by showing one person sacrificing for another. The motto of many writers is "Show, don't tell." Hemingway *shows* his readers love or hate or irony rather than writing "He loved her" or "She hated him" or "He thought she loved him, but she loved another man."

The Style of the Journalist

As a reporter for the *Kansas City Star* newspaper, Hemingway learned the newspaper's writing style. The editor urged journalists to write clearly and simply, using as few words as possible. A good writer uses all five of the senses in writing— sight, hearing, smell, touch, and taste. The facts of an event are mixed with the writer's impressions or feelings about the event. This forces the writer to find the perfect word and not fill the page with unnecessary, distracting words. Journalism is at the root of Ernest Hemingway's writing, and he practiced the techniques he learned at the *Star* and other publications throughout his life.

Hemingway's stories are full of simple sentences that carry much weight. The first sentence of "Big Two-Hearted River" is this: "The train went on up the track out of sight, around one of the hills of burnt timber."[8] It appears to be a simple sentence describing a simple scene, but after carefully reading the whole story, that simple sentence reveals strong emotions.

symbol
Something that represents or suggests another person or thing.

Nick Adams, the character in the story, is left in the wild. The train is a symbol of the modern world. A symbol is something that represents or suggests another idea or thing. The wilderness is uncivilized, wild, and a memory from Nick's past. "He felt he had left everything behind, the need for thinking, the need to write, other needs. It was all back to him."[9] Even the town that used to be where Nick is has been burned to the ground. Nick knew the area when old buildings still stood along the one street of the small town. Things have changed, and now he is returning to nature.

More than the little town has changed, however. The careful reader finds out that Nick has changed as well. It will be interesting to see how Nick handles things now that the train has pulled out of sight. The land is not the same, and he is not the same.

Life and emotions are complex. Ernest Hemingway writes about the complexities of life, but he writes about them in simple, straightforward language. Hemingway poured an incredible amount of effort into his writing, but he left much work for the reader. Although Hemingway uses simple words and sentences, the reader must constantly ask, "Why did that character do that?" or "Why is the timber burnt?" It may take some thought to find an answer, but that answer will prove to be much bigger than the little sentence from which it came.

When Hemingway was a journalist, the fastest way to send information was by telephone, but telephones were not always easy to find. He would often send facts from a news event by telegram. Telegram writers had to pay a certain amount per word, so the messages sent were kept as short as possible, and the receiver of the telegram would add more words to create a whole news article. Hemingway sent many telegrams as a journalist, which put him in the habit of cutting out unnecessary words.

From Oak Park to Paris and Beyond: The Making of the Writer

Ernest Miller Hemingway was born on July 21, 1899, in Oak Park, Illinois, and died in 1961 in Ketchum, Idaho. In 1899, William McKinley was president of the United States, the Spanish-American War was being fought, the diesel engine had just been invented, and Sir Arthur Conan Doyle had recently published his first Sherlock Holmes story. In 1961, John F. Kennedy was president, the Vietnam War was being fought, industrial lasers were being used, and Robert A. Heinlein had just published his science fiction novel *Stranger in a Strange Land*. These two eras were different in many ways. Ernest Hemingway is considered a modern writer, but his writing is not totally separated from what was published in 1899 and before.

Hemingway's mother, Grace, had wanted to be an opera singer, but instead she managed the house and gave music lessons. His father, Clarence, was a medical doctor who enjoyed fishing and studying the outdoors. Ernest Hemingway's grandfathers Anson T. Hemingway and Ernest Hall were both Civil War veterans. Clarence and Grace were very religious and strict parents. They also taught Ernest how to have fun in nature.

When Ernest was only one year old, his parents took him to their vacation house in northern Michigan, on Walloon Lake. There, the young boy showed an interest in outdoor activities. He loved to ride in the family rowboat and eat fish caught by his father. He carried these interests throughout his life. Ernest and his family returned to northern Michigan for many summers.

Ernest Hemingway's Youth

As a toddler, Ernest showed no fear of exploring the lake property. There is a family story that he tripped while running with a stick in his mouth one summer. The stick poked the

Clarence and Grace Hemingway with their children: Ursula (*left*), Ernest (*middle*), and Marcelline (*right*).

back of his throat, and his father had to act fast to take care of the serious wound. This was one of many serious injuries he would face in his lifetime. At age five, when Ernest was asked what he was afraid of, he answered, "'fraid a nothing!"[1]

Ernest had an older sister, Marcelline; three younger sisters, Ursula, Madelaine, and Carol; and a younger brother, Leicester. It seems he gave almost everyone in the Hemingway family a nickname. Ernest called himself Pawnee Bill or Nurnie, Ursula was called Mr. Gigs, Madelaine was called Sunny, and Leicester was called The Pest. Years later, he gave his own children interesting nicknames, such as Bumby and Gigs.

Clarence Hemingway established the Oak Park, Illinois, Agassiz Club. It was an organization that taught boys about nature and Christianity. While the local boys were out on an expedition to study moss or mushrooms, Clarence taught them that all things are created by God and that God is more powerful than any other force. These ideas can be found in Ernest Hemingway's writing, although his characters do not attend church service or abide by the Bible.

A story he wrote titled "A Natural History of the Dead" contains the tale of Mungo Park. He was an adventurer who found himself wandering across an African desert—thirsty, naked, and about to die. Then Park saw a tiny flower growing in the sand. He thought that since God put that flower there and made sure it lived, then God would want him to live too. Park forced himself to keep on walking, and he at last came to a village and was saved.

In the story, Hemingway compares the tale of Mungo Park to the tale of a person studying people killed in war. The tiny flower inspired Mungo Park to survive, but studying the dead leads the observer to think that war is unnatural and terrible.

Hemingway takes Mungo Park's story and makes it modern. In the Agassiz "classes" Clarence Hemingway taught, the boys thought like Mungo Park. War is made by humans and not by nature. Nature is to be admired, and humans are to be feared. The idea that people are not perfect and are sometimes very bad appears in many of Hemingway's stories and books.

Hemingway the Student

In school, Ernest showed an early interest in reading and writing. He read everything from William Shakespeare, Jack London, and Mark Twain to articles in the Chicago newspapers. He also started writing short stories based on what his grandfather Anson told him and what he experienced during his summers in Michigan. Although Ernest had a hard time in his Latin and math classes, his English teachers praised his

THE GREAT WAR

World War I began in June of 1914 when Archduke Franz Ferdinand of Austria was assassinated by a man with ties to a Serbian terrorist group. This led Austria to declare war on Serbia. Other European nations quickly chose sides and the conflict grew rapidly. The United States entered the war in 1917, after German submarines began sinking unarmed American ships. While each side expected a quick victory, the war lasted more than four years and took the lives of nearly ten million people.

Fighting in Italy was considered to be on the Eastern front, and Italy suffered some large defeats at Gorizia and Caporetto. The defeat at Caporetto in 1917 is fictionalized in Hemingway's novel *A Farewell to Arms* and is the most tragic event in Italian military history. Hemingway's portrayal of the Italian retreat at Caporetto is considered to be some of his best writing.

Hemingway circa 1917 (about age eighteen), ready to see what adventures Europe had in store for him.

enthusiasm. He also wrote for his school newspaper, called *Trapeze*, and the yearbook, *Tabula*. All great artists start out doing small things; what they become world famous for would not exist without small projects and hard work.

Ernest was also a good athlete. He joined the high school track, swim, and football teams. On the weekends, he loved hunting, hiking, and boxing. His eyesight was not great, but he was strong and worked hard to learn the best way to do things. When he was a senior in high school, Ernest weighed 150 pounds (68 kilograms) and was nearly 6 feet (182 centimeters) tall.

After graduation from high school, Ernest's father wanted him to go to college, but Ernest was not sure. The year was 1917, and World War I (then called The Great War) was raging in Europe. By 1917, signs of the war had made it to Oak Park, Illinois. Ernest thought about fighting in Europe, and he also thought about taking a job as a reporter for the *Kansas City Star*—at that time one of the largest newspapers in the country. Dr. Hemingway did not want his son to enter the war at the young age of eighteen, and talked with Ernest's uncle Tyler, who lived in Kansas City, about arranging a job interview for Ernest.

Writing for the *Star*

Ernest chose to move to Kansas City. He loved working as a reporter for a big-city newspaper. He worked long hours and wrote stories about criminals and celebrities. Much of what he saw as a reporter would be used in stories much later in his life. It was at the *Star* that Ernest Hemingway formed his writing style.

Working as a reporter for just over six months, Hemingway crafted the writing style that would make him famous. Each reporter was given a copy of "The *Star* Copy Style," which listed the rules for how to write for the newspaper. For example, here are the first four rules: "Use short sentences. Use short first paragraphs. Use vigorous English. Be positive, not negative."[2] There are dozens of other rules. Another rule is "Avoid using 'that' too frequently, but govern use largely by euphony, and strive for smoothness." This means to write so words sound smooth; "euphony" means what sounds good. While he did not follow all these rules in his stories, he did learn how to choose the best word and how to say a lot with only a few words.

Read the following paragraph. Think about what the scene would be like if you were there, right where the story takes place:

> At this time we were working in a shell-smashed house that overlooked the Casa del Campo in Madrid. Below us a battle was being fought. You could see it spread out below you and over the hills, could smell it, could taste the dust of it, and the noise of it was one great slithering sheet of rifle and automatic rifle fire rising and dropping, and in it came the crack of the guns and the bubbly rumbling of the ongoing shells fired from the batteries behind us, the thud of their bursts, and then the rolling yellow clouds of dust.[3]

Hemingway uses "you," implying that you, the reader, could be included in the scene. In this way he involves the reader in the story. He tells us what we can see, smell, taste, and hear. Say "bubbly rumbling" to yourself a few times. A nice rhythm is created; this is euphony. It is probably what Hemingway thought the mortars sounded like.

Instead of writing that a terrible battle was going on, he puts us in the battle and *shows* us what it is like. Also, by writing "at this time," he lets us know that the storyteller has been in situations like this before.

Putting these things together, the reader can more easily imagine being in this story. Getting the reader into the story makes the reader care more about what happens. Here, Hemingway wants us to feel uncomfortable because he wants us to realize that war is dirty, terrible, and scary.

War Over There

In the spring of 1918, after the United States had entered World War I, Hemingway got on a train headed for Chicago and then on to New York. He had volunteered in the Italian Red Cross to serve as an ambulance driver in Italy. He was not accepted into the regular military because of his eyesight, but he really wanted to experience the adventure of battle. Like the United States, Italy was fighting against Germany. His parents were worried about him, but they thought that he would be carrying out Christian duties, so they supported him.

Hemingway saw terrible sights in Italy as an ambulance driver. One of his first duties was to clean up body parts from the scene of a large explosion north of Milan. That made him realize that war is not a game but something that means life or death. He was no longer a kid goofing around in a town near Chicago; he was a man in a war in Italy.

After about one month of service, Hemingway was severely wounded, the first American wounded in Italy during the war. An Austrian mortar shell exploded near him on July 8, 1918, in Fossalta di Piave. The man standing between him and the bomb was killed. Reports state that Hemingway saw a wounded soldier and dragged him to safety. One second later, a round of machine gun fire ripped through his right knee. An

Hemingway recovering from trench mortar wounds in Milan, Italy, 1918.

Italian doctor removed dozens of pieces of shrapnel from his legs and bandaged his knee. Recovery would take five months.

In the hospital in Milan, Italy, Hemingway fell in love with a nurse named Agnes von Kurowsky. She was twenty-four years old, and he was nineteen. The character of Catherine Barkley in Hemingway's novel *A Farewell to Arms* would be based on Nurse von Kurowsky. After Hemingway returned to Oak Park, Illinois, he soon received a letter from von Kurowsky. She was dating another lieutenant.

Hemingway went fishing in Michigan with a few friends and, when he told his war stories at a public library, he met a woman from Toronto, Canada. She invited him to live in her house in Toronto while she went on vacation, and he accepted. He was always searching for adventure, and Toronto sounded more exciting than going back to his hometown.

Hemingway was soon hired as a reporter for the *Toronto Star Weekly* newspaper. He wrote general interest articles such as "The Best Rainbow Trout Fishing" and "Living on $1,000 a Year in Paris." Again, his experiences as a journalist affected his entire writing career. He met many journalists in Toronto he would stay friends with the rest of his life. Eventually he returned to Illinois, this time to Chicago. At a party there, he met a beautiful young woman named Hadley Richardson. They were married on September 3, 1921.

Hemingway was then offered the position of foreign correspondent for the *Toronto Star* newspaper. This meant that the paper would pay for him to go to France, where he would write articles about what was going on in Europe and send them to the newspaper. One of his writer friends gave him the names of other writers there, and the Hemingways set out for Paris. Like his work as a reporter in Kansas City, Hemingway's time in Paris would forever change his life.

Ezra Pound was another mentor to Ernest Hemingway in Paris. The two friends respected each other's work and traveled together.

Paris in the Twenties

In Paris, Hemingway met Ezra Pound and Gertrude Stein, two American writers who helped him a great deal. Pound was a very serious poet who revolutionized poetry by forgetting rhyme and focusing on images in as few words as possible. Stein was a poet and novelist who focused on the sounds of words and creating a mood rather than telling a story. Hemingway often went to Stein's apartment to talk about writing and art. Her apartment was full of great paintings. They looked at the paintings, and Hemingway decided that he had to write like great painters paint. Paul Cézanne was a French painter who used simple colors and brush strokes to create wonderful paintings. Hemingway thought that he should work to write one true sentence and then another and another.

A RENAISSANCE MAN

A Renaissance man (or woman) is someone who has knowledge about and talent in many different things. For example, Ernest Hemingway was a Renaissance man. He could speak several languages, box with great skill, discuss ancient Greek philosophers, and fly-fish like an expert. Hemingway could do those things, and he could talk with scholars and manual laborers alike. He travelled the world and met people from all walks of life.

The Renaissance was a time of highly increased interest in the arts in Europe starting in the fourteenth century. It was a time of interest in learning in many areas (the sciences, art, travel, history), and, although the Renaissance was several centuries ago, one can be considered a Renaissance man or woman even today.

Hemingway thought he could create wonderful stories the same way Cézanne created his paintings. In a book he wrote, which was not published until after his death, Hemingway discusses what he did when he did not know what to write. He told himself, "All you have to do is write one true sentence. Write the truest sentence you know." So finally, I could write one true sentence, and then go on from there. It was easy because there was always one true sentence that I knew or had seen or had heard someone say."[4] This is great advice for any writer. Write one sentence that you think is totally true, and then continue from there, showing what makes it true or why you think it is true.

While Hemingway continued sending articles to the *Toronto Star*, he began writing poetry and short stories. Here is an example of his "one true sentence" idea:

> I have stood on the crowded back platform of a seven o'clock Batignolles bus as it lurched along the wet lamp lit street while men who were going home to supper never looked up from their newspapers as we passed Notre Dame grey and dripping in the rain.[5]

This is just one sentence, but it tells as much as some entire stories. Readers can see the wet streets, hear the rain, and feel the crowded bus. Notre Dame is a huge, famous cathedral in Paris, but people are hurrying home instead of looking at the awesome building. Words like "Batignolles" and "lurched" give the reader deep impressions that they can imagine. I might not know what Batignolles is, but it sounds foreign, like something that would only be understood by people who have been there. "Lurched" feels like something moving not smoothly but bumpy and uncomfortable, as if it were heavy. The words in Hemingway's sentence are straightforward and clear, but the reader can easily add feeling and sense to these words.

Hemingway the Man

Ernest Hemingway had always been a strong, big person, and he became a very good boxer. He practiced boxing and fought with anyone who wanted to box. He attended many fights and met boxers and their trainers. Like all of his experiences, Hemingway's boxing knowledge would be used in his writing. Famous people he met at Gertrude Stein's apartment enjoyed talking with him about writing, art, and boxing. Hemingway seemed to know a little about everything, and he was eager to learn more and more.

The newspaper sent Hemingway to many foreign places, and he caught a serious disease called malaria on one trip. He recovered and continued writing for the newspaper and for himself. In 1922, when Hemingway was on a boring assignment in Switzerland, his wife Hadley got on a train to surprise him. She decided to pack all of his stories and poems in a suitcase so he could work on them. To her horror, the suitcase was stolen at the train station in France. The contents of that suitcase would be priceless now, but the stories and poems have never been found.

Despite his devastation at this huge loss, Hemingway continued to peck out news articles, stories, and poems on his typewriter. He seems to have seen himself as mainly a poet at this time.

The Hemingways traveled throughout Europe, and, in Spain, Hemingway fell in love with the sport of bullfighting. He even took part in a bullfight. In early August of 1923, Ernest Hemingway had his first book published—a thin collection titled *Three Stories and Ten Poems*. While the book was hardly read in America, having his poetry and fiction in print gave him much confidence.

Ernest and Hadley returned briefly to Toronto, where Hadley gave birth to their first child—a son they named John Hadley Nicanor Hemingway. Nicanor was the first name of a bullfighter Hemingway admired. After a few trips to Spain to participate in the famous festival (or *fería*) in Pamplona, Hemingway knew he wanted to write about Spain. He would later write about his experiences at the fería in his book *The Sun Also Rises*.

In addition to the lost suitcase and the birth of his son, a third thing happened to Ernest Hemingway in 1923 that changed his life. After receiving rejections from many publishers, a collection of his short stories titled *in our time* was published. These stories were published again in 1925 with a few more stories and titled *In Our Time*. His book proved to the world that Hemingway was a writer to watch. His writing style was not like any other writer's, although many would later copy his style. Hemingway had established a new kind of writing.

THE MODERN SHORT STORY COLLECTION: *IN OUR TIME*

In Our Time was an unusual book for its time and is still unusual in ours. Each chapter is a short story, and in between each story is a short little scene. These scenes are called vignettes or "interchapters." A vignette is a short piece of descriptive writing, and each one in *In Our Time* presents a scene of violence or the threat of violence. They take place in many parts of the world, and each has an ending that does not let the reader know exactly what will happen, a device often found in modernism. These "open" endings are used in just about everything Hemingway wrote. He does not tell the reader what these brutal scenes mean. The reader has to think about them carefully and think about what emotions they trigger. The reader has to act as a detective, looking at each part of the interchapter as a clue leading to a hidden meaning.

Think about this interchapter:

> Maera lay still, his head on his arms, his face in the sand. He felt warm and sticky from the bleeding. Each time he felt the horn coming. Sometimes the bull only bumped him with his head. Once the horn went all the way through him and he felt it go into the sand[...]Maera wanted to say something and he found he

vignette
A short piece of descriptive writing that shows one moment, a scene without a traditional ending.

could not talk. Maera felt everything getting larger and larger and then smaller and smaller. Then it got larger and larger and then smaller and smaller. Then everything commenced to run faster and faster as when they speed up a cinematograph film. Then he was dead.[1]

At first a reader might think, "So what?" But a closer look reveals more about this short scene. The voice telling this story is not the bullfighter Maera, but the storyteller who knows how Maera feels and what he thinks. This could never happen in life—only in literature. Also, the writing is without emotion. Hemingway does not tell us that the goring hurts,

Hemingway was fascinated by the art of bullfighting and wrote about the sport in *Death in the Afternoon*. He took this photograph of matador Manuel Granero, who was killed later that day in a bullfight in Madrid.

but we can feel the hurt as we think about a bull's horn going completely through our bodies. In addition, Maera is lying face down in the sand. He is completely powerless, extremely uncomfortable, and cannot see what is going on. He cannot speak either.

What does Maera want to say? Was he a good person? Hemingway does not answer these questions, but readers can answer them for themselves. It is possible to see a bullfight from the grandstand, and some people get to see bullfights from the perspective of a bullfighter. But no one knows what happens to a dying bullfighter. Hemingway imagined what it would be like, but he left room for readers to fill in their own ideas. Imagine feeling a bull's wet breath on the back of your head and the huge crowd screaming. Imagine your face in the sand. Imagine the shrinking and expanding, the speeding up.

Then Hemingway gets back to the storyteller's voice and tells us, "Then he was dead." What happens then? No one knows, but readers can imagine.

In Our Time contains many scenes of suffering, death, drunkenness, and dark courage. In addition, the endings of the stories do not leave the reader feeling satisfied and happy. The interchapter titled "L'Envoi" involves a king talking about how he is glad a general has some soldiers shot. The king wishes another general would have had more men shot. Then Hemingway writes, "It was very jolly. We talked for a long time. Like all Greeks he wanted to go to America."[2] This is an example of irony. It is ironic because there really is nothing jolly about killing. Killing is very serious and sad, and not all generals are brave heroes. Hemingway uses irony here to show how powerful leaders can forget that war and killing are not simply parts of a game. Real people are involved, and these people have lives and feelings. Hemingway knew about soldiers and also about generals and world leaders. He knew the suffering that soldiers go through, and he wanted his readers to understand that, too.

This interchapter is also ironic in another way. The king of Greece cannot leave the palace grounds because he has been overthrown by revolutionary soldiers. He is giving military advice while his military leadership has fallen apart. In addition, the fact that the king of Greece wants to go to America is ironic. The king should stay and rule his land. Looking at the evidence Hemingway has planted, we realize that the king of Greece in this interchapter is a bad leader.

Introducing Nick Adams

In his book *In Our Time*, Ernest Hemingway introduces the character Nick Adams. As Hemingway biographer James R. Mellow writes, "The invention of Nick Adams was one of the most vital inspirations of Hemingway's career."[3]

Although Nick Adams is only an invented character, he has many of the same experiences Hemingway had. Living in Paris and traveling throughout Europe, Hemingway met many interesting and important people. At one time or another, it seems he made almost all of these people mad at him by writing stories about them. Hemingway changed the people's names in the stories, but most people knew who the embarrassing stories were about.

Because of this, Hemingway had many acquaintances but few close, true friends. Like the character Nick Adams, he was a man alone in a crowd. Nick Adams did not have a whole lot of friends, but he wasn't hated, either. This was how the modern person was: individual, unique, and thoughtful, but also part of the crowd. He did what he thought was right, and he admitted when he was wrong. He took someone's advice only when he felt it was the right thing to do. These were Nick Adams's principles. This was his code.

The Code Hero

Nick Adams and a few of Hemingway's other characters have been called "code heroes" by those who study literature. Nick is driven to do what he thinks is right. He is not very concerned with what others say or how other characters tell him to live. The code hero is a character who is confident in his beliefs and who trusts himself as a guide rather than letting others tell him what to do. A person's code is that person's principles or morals. If a character does not break his or her code, then that character is a hero. The code hero, one type of Hemingway character, is confident in his beliefs and shows grace under pressure. He also suffers because of his code.

The character Nick Adams follows a code. Hemingway wrote about Nick Adams in many stories. Nick travels to places Hemingway traveled to, and Nick meets the people Hemingway met (although their names are changed). Nick Adams first appears in a very short story called "Did You Ever Kill Anyone?" That story takes place in World War I, and Nick is wounded much as Hemingway was wounded in Italy. In the story "Indian Camp," Nick and his father are in an area very much like the one Hemingway and his father visited in Michigan. In the story, as in real life, the father is a doctor.

In "Indian Camp" and a few other stories about Nick Adams when he is young, Nick is not really a code hero because he has not lived long enough to establish a code. It takes experience for a person to develop a set of morals by which to live, and young Nick

code hero

A type of Hemingway character who is confident in his beliefs and shows "grace under pressure."

is just beginning to develop his code. In these stories, Nick's father is helping Nick make his code.

"Indian Camp" is the first story Hemingway wrote with Nick Adams as a character. While Hemingway wrote in a modern style, many of his themes are not new. The notion of a father showing his son how beautiful and unfair life can be is very old. As Hemingway biographer David Wyatt writes, as they set out to an Indian camp in a canoe, "The acute sense of setting out also quickly reveals itself as a journey back, into American origins."[4] This is part of the strength of Hemingway's writing—the ability to smoothly combine the new with the old.

theme

A distinctive concern or idea that is prevalent in a work of fiction.

All the stories that feature Nick Adams show that he does not really fit in with the people around him. However, Nick does not seem to be troubled by that fact. He has a very good idea of who he is, or maybe he just decides what kind of person he wants to be, and everything he does makes him become that kind of person. He knows his strengths and weaknesses, and he tries to be honest and fair. In these respects, he is very similar to Hemingway.

In some stories (like "Indian Camp"), Nick is a boy, and in many more stories he is a man. Hemingway considered his story "Big Two-Hearted River" to be the best one about Nick Adams. It is included in *In Our Time*, and Hemingway wrote it when he was twenty-five years old. "Big Two-Hearted River" is a memorable, and even incredible, story. It might be the best example of how Hemingway's iceberg theory can be used to create a deeply meaningful story without much action.

Seizing the Moment

Another aspect of the Hemingway hero is his distrust in anything but the here and now. The soldiers and bullfighters in Hemingway's fiction know that they might die at any time. They also recognize that people change throughout life. What seemed certain once might seem very different now; memory cannot be trusted. The only thing that can be trusted is the present moment.

In *For Whom the Bell Tolls*, Maria asks Robert Jordan if he loves her. He answers, "Yes, I love you now . . . thou art

Ingrid Bergman as Maria and Gary Cooper as Roberto at the trigger of "el máquina" in the 1943 film version of *For Whom the Bell Tolls*.

45

my woman now."[5] Jordan later thinks, "You have it now and that is all your whole life is; now. There is nothing else than now. There is neither yesterday, certainly, nor is there any tomorrow. How old must you be before you know that? There is only now."[6] These characters enjoy eating, drinking, and enjoying life because of the dark cloud of death that always hovers near. They know that the past cannot be changed and that it does no good to worry about things in the future that cannot be changed.

The Complex Simple Things

When Hemingway was making notes for his novel *A Farewell to Arms*, he jotted down a conversation between the main character (a lieutenant) and a priest. This is different from the version that was published in the book, but this first draft shows how this soldier appreciates things that affect his five senses rather than things that are more complex and sophisticated.

[The Priest asks,] "You don't love anything?"

[Lieutenant Henry answers,] "Yes, I love a lot of things.

"What are they?"

"I don't know. Lots of things."

"What?"

I thought a minute.

"The night. The day. Food. Drink. Girls. Italy. Pictures. Places. Swimming. Portofino. Paris. Spring. Summer. Fall. Winter. Heat. Cold. Smells. Sleep. Newspapers. Reading."[7]

Portofino is a type of wine. The things the soldier likes are things that touch the five senses: sight, hearing, smell, touch, and taste.

The River and the Swamp

There is very little action in "Big Two-Hearted River," but there is much to entertain the five senses. Nick hikes alone to the river, takes a nap, sets up his tent, sleeps, wakes up, eats, fishes, and goes back to his tent. The sentences in the story are short, and almost all of the words are simple.

Hemingway seems to have followed the *Kansas City Star* writing rules when he wrote this story. The reader can only guess where Nick came from and why he is there. It seems that fishing is not the main reason for Nick to go on this trip. It seems like he does it to clear his head and to be alone. When he gets off the train, the land is black from a recent forest fire. However, by the river, things are green and alive. This could symbolize Nick's life. What he is leaving is dead, and he is going toward life. Nick is wearing a military-style shirt, and, in his book *A Moveable Feast*, Hemingway wrote that "The story was about coming back from the war but there was no mention of the war in it."[8]

Performing the jobs of setting up camp, cooking, and fishing make Nick feel good because he is in control of what he does. He can do whatever he wants to do. He pours both a can of pork and beans and a can of spaghetti into the frying pan. "I've got a right to eat this kind of stuff, if I'm willing to carry it," Nick says to himself.[9]

This makes the reader think that Nick had previously been in some situation where he was not in control of what he could do. Because the fictional life of Nick Adams is so much like the real life of Ernest Hemingway, it may be that Nick has returned injured from the war and gone fishing to feel both better and more in control. Many of Hemingway's characters are in bad situations like war, but they do what they can to control as much of their lives as they can.

While the short story seems to go nowhere, it really tells a lot about Nick Adams. The reader has to take the evidence Hemingway gives and discover what it all means. Gertrude Stein had taught Hemingway that the writer should not tell too much; the reader should use imagination and logic to fill in any gaps in a story.

The Demands of the Code

The idea of a character sticking to his or her code sometimes leads to conflicts with other characters. Sticking to a code could even mean breaking a law. There is a famous scene in *A Farewell to Arms* that shows the Italian retreat at Caporetto. The army had to move back because they were being beaten by enemy forces. The scene (covering chapters 28 to 31) shows what war is really like from the soldier's perspective.

In this memorable scene, Frederic Henry asks two fellow soldiers to help him get the car out from the mud. The soldiers refuse, and Henry shoots one of the soldiers. This seems like a terrible thing to do, but Frederic Henry does it because those two soldiers are not doing their duty. They refused to obey Henry, and the punishment for such behavior is death. Henry does not enjoy doing this, but he has to.

The Code and Isolation

Maintaining a code sometimes means isolating yourself from others. Hemingway calls this a "separate peace." In *A Farewell to Arms*, Frederic Henry thinks, "I had the paper but I did not read it because I did not want to read about the war.

I was going to forget the war. I had made a separate peace."[10] He has accepted his situation and found a different way to peace in wartime.

There is a one-page scene in *In Our Time* in which Nick Adams is sitting against a church wall. It is during a battle. Next to Nick is his friend Rinaldi, but Rinaldi is lying face-down, seriously injured. Nick is also injured—he was hit in the spine. He says to Rinaldi, "You and me we've made a separate peace."[11] This line looks simple, but it could be very complex. Like an iceberg, we see the simple sentence, but more is hidden below the surface, and the reader has to think about what that bigger part below might be.

Clearly, there is not peace around them. Peace might mean the end of war, but Nick and Rinaldi might have found a different kind of peace. Maybe they fear they are going to die, so they prayed to God. That could be a separate peace. Or maybe they have realized that fighting is not the best solution to whatever problems both sides of the battle are having. If they have decided to give up fighting, they have found a separate peace that way. The war would continue, but they have made peace for themselves. Or maybe they will not be able to fight in the war because of their injuries. If they cannot fight, then they have made peace that way.

"The Killers"

Another famous story featuring Nick Adams is "The Killers," published in 1927. Readers today might be surprised that Hemingway used the word "nigger" in the story to refer to the African-American cook. Hemingway did that because that is what people in a diner in the outskirts of Chicago would have said in the 1920's. It is important to realize the characters call the cook that, but the narrator (who also represents Hemingway's voice) calls him "the cook." The word was offensive even then, but some people used it anyway.

Two professional killers come to the diner looking for Ole Anderson, a former professional boxer. They know he goes to the diner a lot, so they tie up the cook and Nick Adams, who is a customer, and wait for Ole Anderson. He does not come to the diner, and the killers leave. Despite the danger, Nick decides to tell Anderson the killers are looking for him, but Anderson does nothing to avoid this certain death. Nick seems to be the only character who is concerned.

Boxing is a violent sport. The landlady where Ole lives says he does not act like a boxer. "You'd never know it except from the way his face is. . . . He's just as gentle."[12] Ole Anderson's face must look like he got hit a lot. A successful boxer would not get hit that much and would probably have enough money to buy a house.

Hemingway tells us Ole Anderson was a "heavyweight prizefighter." Therefore, we can guess his last years as a boxer were not good ones. He was once a great boxer, but now he is nobody special. It seems that Ole Anderson accepts violence in life and is willing to pay the ultimate price for some mistake he made. He gives up.

Anderson feels he has to suffer for what he did, and he waits for the men to kill him. He feels like his life is ready to be over. Although the story is called "The Killers," it is more about how Nick Adams feels about Ole Anderson and the other characters. Nick cannot believe they do not want to try to stop the killing. The other characters have been in the town longer than Nick has, and they accept what is going on. Nick is new to the town, and he wants to leave. Nick does not want to become another person who accepts tragedy.

Elizabeth "Hadley" Richardson and Ernest Hemingway on their wedding day, September 3, 1921, at Horton Bay, Michigan. They were married a little over five years and had one child, Jack.

"Indian Camp"

A younger Nick Adams appears in the story "Indian Camp," from *In Our Time*. In this story, we learn that Nick's father is a doctor, just like Hemingway's was in real life. Nick, his father, and his uncle go to a cabin where a Native American woman is about to give birth. Dr. Adams helps with the delivery as the woman's husband waits in a bunk bed over the woman. The woman is screaming because the baby will not come out. Dr. Adams has to perform an operation to help the baby out. Nick does not watch this.

When the baby is born, Nick watches his father take a blanket off the husband on the upper bunk. Nick and his father see that the man has killed himself by cutting his throat. They talk about it on the way back to their cabin. The story ends, "In the early morning on the lake sitting in the stern of the boat with his father rowing, he felt quite sure that he would never die."[13]

Just like in "The Killers," Nick Adams refuses to give into the feeling that life is unfair. His father says the husband killed himself because "he couldn't stand things."[14] Nick thinks he is stronger than that; that he will be able to stand things. Even at his young age, Nick understands that life is unpredictable. He believes that he will never die because he thinks he is tough enough to make his life what he wants it to be.

It is interesting to compare the young Nick Adams in "Indian Camp" to the older, more experienced Nick Adams in "Big Two-Hearted River." "Indian Camp" is the second story in *In Our Time*, and "Big Two-Hearted River" is the last. In "Big Two-Hearted River," Nick does not want to fish in the deep swamp because "the fishing would be tragic. In the swamp fishing was a tragic adventure. Nick did not want it."[15] This older Nick no longer feels as if he will live forever. He knows that he has to be careful.

The beauty of simple writing is that the reader can make up his or her own meaning. One reader can think it means one thing, and another reader can think it means something else. Both readers can be right.

Fame Comes to Hemingway

After the publication of *In Our Time*, Hemingway still wrote some poetry, but he liked writing short stories much more.

Publishers thought *In Our Time* was shocking when they first read it because of the violence and rough language in some scenes. Hemingway changed a few things, and the book was released by a larger publishing company in October 1925. Several large magazines and newspapers wrote about his book, and the interest immediately made Hemingway a famous writer.

Papa

People liked how the iceberg theory worked in Hemingway's stories to make realistic characters. His writing style was compared to the artistic style of famous painters like Pablo Picasso.

F. Scott Fitzgerald, Gertrude Stein, *Time* magazine, the *New York Times* newspaper, and many other people and publications could tell that Hemingway was going to be a great writer. Hemingway also became a close friend to fellow author F. Scott Fitzgerald. Hemingway loved his new popularity, and he met many more important people in Paris. People who met him were impressed with his honest style, his strength, his war stories, and his knowledge of literature.

Ernest and Hadley Hemingway went to many parties and traveled throughout Europe having fun. Hemingway's tall, strong body and his confident attitude earned him the nickname "Papa." In a short time, people around the world would know who Papa was.

THE GREAT CYCLE OF LIFE: *THE SUN ALSO RISES*: BUMMING AROUND EUROPE

rnest Hemingway never seemed to write what he thought people wanted just to get rich and famous. His writing has a unique tone and feel. He managed to make old themes new and his own, and he developed a large audience of readers who found his writing to be powerful. As Hemingway became more and more popular, he appeared to feel more confident about writing what he thought of the world. He saw bad things happening to good people, including himself. After seeing what war was like, suffering lost love, and living the life of an American in Paris, Hemingway began to feel there was much futility in life.

Futility is the feeling of helplessness; a feeling that results cannot be predicted or expected. Hemingway's writings all communicate that humans cannot really control what happens to them. Sometimes good people die young, and sometimes bad people live long lives. Since this is true, all people can do is enjoy life and try to be good. This is the main idea of the Lost Generation. It would also become one of the primary themes of Hemingway's classic novel, *The Sun Also Rises*. There is hope, however. After all, the sun rises as well as sets. It is the great circle of life.

Consider for a moment the short story, "Cross Country Snow." In this story, Nick Adams and his friend George have

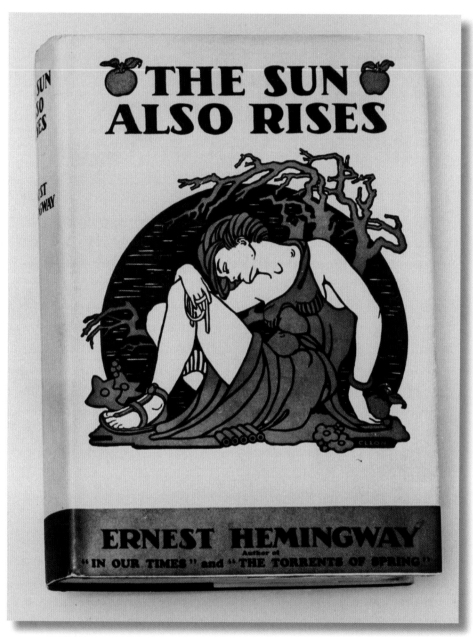

A first edition of *The Sun Also Rises*. Hemingway wrote the book in an incredible two months in 1925. A true first edition now is worth over $20,000 to collectors.

a great time skiing in Switzerland. They take a break at a lodge house and talk. George may have to move back to the United States, and Nick is worried that they will not get to ski together again.

> "Maybe we'll never go skiing again, Nick," George said.
>
> "We've got to," said Nick. "It isn't worth while if you can't."
>
> "We'll go, all right," George said. "We've got to," Nick agreed.
>
> "I wish we could make a promise about it," George said.
>
> Nick stood up. He buckled his wind jacket tight. He leaned over George and picked up the two ski poles from against the wall. He stuck one of the ski poles into the floor.
>
> "There isn't any good in promising," he said.[1]

At that moment Nick does not think life is worth living if you cannot ski. He also realizes it is no use to promise that they will ski together again because he has no idea what the future will bring. They can promise to ski again, but that does not mean they will be able to ski next year. You can hope to ski, but it is not certain.

The two friends do get to ski down the rest of the mountain, though. At the end of "Cross Country Snow," Hemingway writes, "Nick put on his gloves. George was already started up the road, his skis on his shoulder. Now they would have the run home together."[2] They cannot promise what the future will bring, but they will ski together now. Now is all they can count on.

When Nick Adams sets up camp at the Big Two-Hearted River, he remembers a friend of his named Hopkins. He was camping with Hopkins and another friend on the Black River when news came that oil was discovered on land Hopkins owned. The three friends decided that they would fish again the next year and take a yacht cruise along the north shore of Lake Superior. Then Nick realizes that he never saw Hopkins again. It was futile to make plans to go fishing and cruising. His memory of Hopkins is not sad, though. Nick still makes coffee the way Hopkins used to when they went camping. Nick laughs because the coffee turns out too bitter to drink.

Nick is afraid to fish the swamp, but he tells himself, "There were plenty of days coming when he could fish the swamp."[3] This thought, however, could prove to be futile. There is a chance he will never get to fish the swamp. Still, he likes to think that he will. That is his hope.

"Nada" and the Night

Futility is the basis for nihilism. Nihilism is the belief that human existence is completely pointless and useless. True nihilism is the belief that God, manners, property, marriage, morality, and other things made by society have no real value. Hemingway was not a true nihilist. He very much believed in the importance of manners and morals. Some readers think he was a nihilist because of some instances in his stories when a character questions the point of life.

The old waiter in "A Clean, Well-Lighted Place" talks to himself as he walks home very late at night. He has a sense of fear, but he cannot figure out what it is he fears. Hemingway writes, "What did he fear? It was not fear or dread. It was a nothing that he knew too well. It was all a nothing and a man was nothing too."[4] The old waiter thinks a clean, well-lighted place where a person can be treated with respect is very important. The young waiter cannot understand this. The old waiter values dignity very highly, but the young waiter cannot see the dignity in people. Dignity and respect are the only things that matter to the old waiter. He developed this attitude from his life experiences, but he is not a true nihilist. He values the happiness of others over his own happiness.

Another part of "A Clean, Well-Lighted Place" that confuses many readers is what the old waiter thinks next on his way home. He thinks of prayers, but he changes the words to suit his mood:

> Some lived in it and never felt it [a feeling of emptiness] but he knew it all was nada y pues nada y nada y pues nada. Our nada who art in nada, nada be thy name thy kingdom nada thy will be nada in nada as it is in nada. Give us this nada our daily nada and nada us our nada as we nada our nadas.[5]

"Nada y pues nada" means "nothing and for nothing" in Spanish. The old waiter feels that even prayers mean nothing. He probably learned the prayers growing up, but the religion of his youth is not working for the older man. He carries some Christian values (like helping those in need and treating people fairly), but he thinks the prayers are worthless. The old waiter's principles are misunderstood, and he feels like a stranger.

The Sun Also Rises

Hadley and Ernest Hemingway vacationed in Spain for the third time in the summer of 1925. They went to bullfights and spent many nights drinking Spanish wine. They stayed all summer, and Ernest jotted down in notebooks interesting words or sentences he heard. He knew from the start how he wanted to write about their experiences in Spain. He had some success with his early short stories, but he wanted to write a novel. In a novel, he could tell one long story and also slip in smaller stories. He could also write more about the characters.

He started typing the novel while on vacation in Northern Spain. Then he and Hadley went to a resort town in France where he continued writing in notebooks. In one month, Ernest Hemingway had written over 250 notebook pages, and he finished writing his novel *Fiesta* in Paris on September 21, 1925. The entire book is about his experiences with friends in the city of Pamplona, in Northern Spain. He changed the names of the characters, but it is easy to figure out which of his friends is a character in the book.

Hemingway did not like the title *Fiesta*, and he thought of changing it to *The Lost Generation* because of the story about Gertrude Stein and the mechanic. He finally chose to name his first novel *The Sun Also Rises*. He chose that title from the Bible—Ecclesiastes 1:4–5, which reads:

> One generation passeth away, and another generation cometh: but the earth abideth for ever. The sun ariseth, and the sun goeth down, and hasteth to his place where he arose.

The message of the book of Ecclesiastes is that life should be enjoyed but also that things can happen that no one can control. The smartest person can seem like a fool compared to the power of nature. William Shakespeare also used the ideas in Ecclesiastes in a few of his famous plays. Ecclesiastes is very much about the futility of humans and how it is not good always to think of yourself.

This futility is evident in *The Sun Also Rises*. Robert Cohn was a boxing champion in college, but he hates boxing. He really wants to be a writer. The character who tells the story, Jake Barnes, had an injury in the war that left him impotent, which means he can't have children. Jake and Lady Brett Ashley seem to be in love with each other, but they can never really be with each other because of Jake's injury and because Brett is already married. Another of the friends in the novel, Michael Campbell, is in love with Brett. Brett likes a bullfighter named Romero, but she eventually decides to marry Michael once she's divorced her husband.

The relationships of these characters get a little confusing, but they all seem to want something they can't get. They also feel bad about things in the past. They wish they would have done things differently and not been so concerned about themselves. It is too late to change those things now, though, so a person can only try to get things right in the future.

Needing What Can't Be Had

Each of these characters wants something he or she cannot get. No matter how hard they try, they cannot find meaning in their lives. In fact, at the end of the novel, none of the characters has really changed. Many people think the Lost Generation were bad people because they drank too much alcohol, wasted money, and spent too much time at parties instead of at work.

A popular idea about the Lost Generation is that many of these people felt World War I was useless and another sign that people cannot control their destinies. They thought that they might as well have a good time since they could not control the future. The writer F. Scott Fitzgerald wrote about this idea in his book *Tender Is the Night*. In Fitzgerald's book and in *The Sun Also Rises*, characters who live this party life feel lost and unhappy.

The Design of *The Sun Also Rises*

Hemingway asked a few of his friends for advice on the book as he wrote it. F. Scott Fitzgerald suggested a different beginning, and Hemingway took his advice and changed it. Authors almost never write anything in one sitting; they go back and go back, changing and fixing things many times before they think it is good enough to publish.

The Sun Also Rises is divided into three books. The first book introduces Cohn, Brett, and Jake. They are in Paris, all unhappy. What carries this first book is the realistic dialogue. Hemingway reveals much about the characters through dialogue. It is not easy to write what people say and make it seem realistic.

Robert Cohn tells Jake Barnes he is sick of Paris, and he wants to do something else. Jake begins the dialogue:

"I've had plenty to worry about one time or other. I'm through worrying."

"Well, I want to go to South America."

"Listen, Robert, going to another country doesn't make any difference. I've tried all that. You can't get away from yourself by moving from one place to another. There's nothing to that."[6]

F. Scott Fitzgerald (*pictured*) and Hemingway helped each other craft their writing styles after they first met in Paris in 1925.

Actions Behind the Words

The interesting thing about this little bit of dialogue is that it reveals that Jake has been through a bad experience. We learn that he is from Kansas City, so the fact that he is in Paris means that he, himself, has tried going to another country. This is what he tells Cohn not to do. Jake believes that the only way to escape problems is to change the way you think. He claims he has stopped worrying, but he has plenty of worries. That very night he cannot sleep.

> I lay awake thinking and my mind jumping around. Then I couldn't keep away from it [the war experiences], and I started to think about Brett and all the rest of it went away. I was thinking about Brett and my mind stopped jumping around and started to go in sort of smooth waves. Then all of a sudden I started to cry. Then after a while it was better and I lay in bed and listened to the heavy trams go by and way down the street, and then I went to sleep.[7]

Just as moving to another place is no way to escape problems, merely saying you are "through with worrying" does not mean you do not have worries. The only thing that matters is action. Talking about something is useless; you have to do it. This is another idea from the Lost Generation. This is what Brett is talking about when she says, "Let's not talk. Talking's all bilge."[8] Bilge means worthless junk. Nick Adams would agree with Brett. That is why he did not promise to go skiing again with George in "Cross Country Snow."

A Dark Future

The mood or feeling of the ending of *The Sun Also Rises* is much like that of a short story by F. Scott Fitzgerald called "Babylon Revisited." Hemingway thought very highly of Fitzgerald's story. In it, a man locks his wife out of their house one cold winter night because they are both drunk, and he thinks she is interested in another man.

The woman eventually dies from an illness she got from that cold night. Their only child is sent to live with the woman's sister. The man comes back after a couple of years to try to convince his sister-in-law to let him have his daughter back. He has her almost convinced, but a couple of old party friends of his show up and remind the sister-in-law of his drunken past. He does not get custody of his daughter.

The Sun Also Rises is different, though, because we do not know what will happen in the future after Brett and Jake part ways. The reader can assume, however, that there will not be a very happy conclusion. Brett says she will be nice to Mike, but she has made promises before that she did not keep.

The Sun Also Rises ends with Jake and Brett in the back of a taxi. They are going for a ride before Brett returns to Mike. "Oh, Jake," Brett says, "we could have had such a damned good time together." Jake answers, "Isn't it pretty to think so?"[9] This is yet another example of Hemingway's notion of hope within futility. Thinking about something does not change it, but sometimes it is good to just think about things anyway, like Jake did while trying to get to sleep.

Both Brett and Jake know they probably never would have had a good time together because of the kind of people they are. Although Jake may appear to be agreeing that the two of them could have been happy together in different circumstances, it seems doubtful that he really believes this. Or perhaps he is merely recognizing how pointless it is to speculate about what might have been.

Enter Pauline

Immediately after finishing *The Sun Also Rises*, Ernest Hemingway wrote a few more short stories and began writing another novel. This new book was a parody. A parody is humorous writing that makes fun of another book. The book Hemingway was making fun of was *Dark Laughter* by Sherwood Anderson. Hemingway titled it *The Torrents of Spring*. Many of Hemingway's friends thought it was mean to make fun of another writer. Sherwood Anderson said he disliked *The Torrents of Spring*, but he did not mind if Hemingway published it. It was published, but it was not one of his more popular books.

Pauline Pfeiffer, a friend of Hadley, thought the book was very funny. She was an editor for *Vogue* magazine. Hemingway eventually fell in love with Pfeiffer. Hadley Hemingway knew that Ernest loved Pauline, so she said she would grant him a divorce if he and Pauline still loved each other after being separated for one hundred days. As a result, Hemingway spent much of 1926 traveling. F. Scott Fitzgerald helped him polish *The Sun Also Rises* during this time.

parody
A work in which one writer imitates and exaggerates another writer's work.

By the end of the hundred days, Pauline and Ernest did still love each other, and Ernest and Hadley were legally separated. Soon afterward, *The Sun Also Rises* was published. Hemingway dedicated the novel to his wife and son: "This book is for Hadley and for John Hadley Nicanor."

The Sun Also Rises earned Hemingway much money and fame. He traveled with Pauline to Key West, Florida, meeting famous artists along the way. He fished almost every day in

Pauline Pfeiffer and Ernest Hemingway after their 1927 marriage. Pauline was Ernest's second wife. They had two sons, Patrick and Gregory.

Key West. Memories of his fishing adventures later became key parts of another novel. On May 10, 1927, Hemingway and Pauline were married.

A curious accident happened to Ernest Hemingway in March 1928, when he and Pauline were in Paris. He came home after having dinner with some friends, and he went into the bathroom. Toilets in France used to (and many still do) flush by pulling a cord. Hemingway reached for the flushing cord but instead pulled a cord leading to a ceiling skylight. The glass window fell on his head, and the scar left on his forehead is visible in many photographs of him.

Patrick Hemingway was born in the summer of 1928, and Hemingway was already several hundred pages into writing another novel. This one would be called *A Farewell to Arms*.

LOVE AND GUNS: "FRANCIS MACOMBER" AND *A FAREWELL TO ARMS*

In 1925, Ernest Hemingway wrote in a letter to writer F. Scott Fitzgerald that "war is the best subject of all. It groups the maximum of material and speeds up the action and brings out all sorts of stuff that normally you have to wait a lifetime to get."[1] He wanted to fight in World War I because it seemed like it was exciting, and most men his age went to Europe to join the fight. Although he ended up volunteering as an ambulance driver for the American Red Cross, Hemingway saw battle action and got a taste of what war was like. His experiences in World War I provided the background for *A Farewell to Arms*. With his sister Sunny typing for him six hours a day for five weeks, the novel was finished in January 1929.

Hemingway was offered a large amount of money for *A Farewell to Arms*, but his father, Clarence, committed suicide about the same time, so it was a time of mixed emotions. He carefully checked over his writing and rewrote most of the novel before sending it to the publisher. The publisher thought Hemingway used too much bad language in the

Hemingway in the mid-1920s. Success suited this up-and-coming
American novelist in Europe.

book, and Max Perkins, the editor, convinced Hemingway to change or hide the profanity, which he did. The novel quickly became a bestseller.

Hemingway took the title of his book from a poem by George Peele, a writer in the late 1500s. Peele's poem was dedicated to Queen Elizabeth I. It is about an old man who was once a brave soldier. His battle helmet became a home for bees, and his blonde hair became gray. His devotion to the queen, however, remained as strong as ever.

A Farewell to Arms ends without the reader knowing what will happen next to the soldier. Considering the poem, though, the reader might guess that the soldier will continue to fight for what he thinks is right. He will not simply give up, which would be the easy thing to do in his circumstances.

The novel is based on many of Hemingway's own experiences during World War I in Italy. The hero, Frederic Henry, is an American ambulance driver. He suffers an injury very similar to Hemingway's real-life war injury and falls in love with a nurse in an Italian hospital. Hemingway uses the same kind of dialogue that made *The Sun Also Rises* so effective, and he adds other details to make his characters seem perfectly real. James R. Mellow writes, "Each of these characters is well defined, crackling with life."[2]

When readers know a lot about a character, they begin to care about what happens to that character. In *A Farewell to Arms*, we care about Frederic Henry and many other characters, too. Hemingway uses his iceberg principle to give these other details deep meaning. For example, here is a famous passage from the first chapter:

> Troops went by the house and down the road and the dust they raised powdered the leaves of the trees. The trunks of the trees too were dusty and the leaves fell

early that year and we saw the troops marching along
the road and the dust rising and leaves, stirred by the
breeze, falling and the soldiers marching and afterward
the road bare and white except for the leaves.[3]

This passage tells us a lot about how the narrator feels
about what is going on in the story. The dust raised by the
soldiers marching by covers everything, and the leaves fell
early that year. This means that it is not natural. The dust is
rising, and the leaves are falling. The soldiers are marching
down the road, and then they are gone. There is much motion
in these two sentences. Also, the second sentence is very
long. Hemingway did this to connect the marching troops to
the early falling leaves and to give the feeling of a long line
of soldiers as they march along. Therefore, what seems like
nothing more than soldiers marching along means much
more. It sets the tone for the whole novel.

There were mists over the river and clouds on the
mountain and the trucks splashed mud on the road and
the troops were muddy and wet in their capes; their
rifles were wet under their capes and the two leather
cartridge-boxes on the front of their belts, grey leather
boxes heavy with the packs of clips of thin, long 6.5 mm.
cartridges, bulged forward under the capes so that the
men, passing on the road, marched as though they were
six months gone with child.[4]

"Gone with child" means pregnant. Hemingway creates
a wicked image the careful reader can pick up on. Instead of
the beauty and joy of a woman being pregnant, Hemingway
gives us muddy soldiers carrying weapons into war. Instead of
an innocent little baby, the soldiers are carrying things to kill
people. Instead of a nice sunny picture, Hemingway paints a

misty, muddy, and dark picture. The tip of this iceberg is that the leaves fell early that year; the bottom of the iceberg is war, pain, fire, mud, and death.

In the middle of the novel, Frederic Henry says, "I was always embarrassed by the words sacred, glorious, and sacrifice and the expression in vain."[5] This is the same idea as Brett Ashley saying that talk is worthless. Hemingway felt that certain words were misused so often that they had lost their real meaning. People say words all the time without thinking about what they really mean. As a soldier, Frederic Henry is sick of phrases like "a glorious war" or "died in vain." He must wonder if war is really like glory in the Bible or if dying in a war that you don't really believe in is equal to being crucified to save an entire race of people. This idea that words must be used with care runs throughout all of Hemingway's writing.

Frederic Without Catherine

The tragic ending of *A Farewell to Arms* leaves the reader certain that war is terrible. It also makes us feel the futility of modern life. The nurse Frederic Henry falls in love with, Catherine Barkley, is a person who tries to do good. However, in the end, she is not rewarded for her good deeds. Frederic Henry's prayers go unanswered, and he wonders why Catherine is suffering instead of him. He prays not like he would usually pray but how he was probably taught to pray as a boy, and his praying does not seem to do any good. The novel is both soft and rough, nice and cruel, sweet and bitter. And this is how Hemingway felt about war.

This novel was another huge success. Hemingway next began writing a book about bull fighting. He also went hunting and relaxed.

The severe injuries Ernest Hemingway received in his ten months in Africa lasted the rest of his life, but he found the continent thrilling. Here, he is photographed on safari in 1937, holding kudu antelope horns.

Throughout his adult life, Ernest Hemingway suffered many accidents. He had a badly cut eye, the disease anthrax, a fractured skull, a large gash on his forehead, a badly broken arm, blown-up knees, a severely cut leg and finger, gun shots from an accident on his boat, and a ripped chin. But he was generally healthy and remained active, so these injuries did not slow him down.

Pauline's uncle Gus bought a house in Key West, Florida, as a gift to Pauline and Ernest. Before relocating there, the Hemingways went to Kansas City so Pauline could have a baby. Gregory Hancock Hemingway was born on November 12, 1931.

Hemingway finished his book on bullfighting and titled it *Death in the Afternoon*. The book was not well received by reviewers, but it is still one of the most informative books on bullfighting. It is an odd book because it contains many facts and observations about bullfighting, but it also has parts where the narrator talks to an imaginary old woman. These conversations are a little like the interchapters from *In Our Time*.

In 1933, Hemingway traveled to Africa. As usual, his experiences were later made into stories. The most famous stories from his African experiences are "The Short Happy Life of Francis Macomber," "The Snows of Kilimanjaro," and the novel *Green Hills of Africa*. He told people he was happiest when he was writing.

Accident or Murder?

"The Short Happy Life of Francis Macomber" is one of Hemingway's best-known stories. Written in 1936, it is a tale of fear, codes, and justice. In the story, a wealthy American couple, the Macombers, hire a professional hunter to help them on a big-game hunt in Africa. Francis Macomber ends

HEMINGWAY'S HUMOR

While much of Hemingway's writing centers on war, suffering, and other serious topics, he also liked to joke and laugh. This comes through in his letters, which are just now being organized and published for the first time. Here are a few examples of humor in letters he wrote:

To his friend Emily Goetzmann, 1916: "On pended gknees I peg your bardun vor the ladness of this legger. Bud a gombination of monthly examinachugs and Bad goldt are my eggscuse, or to quote 'them immortal lines,' the brooks are ruggig — also my gnose."[6]

To his parents from Italy, 1918: "Don't weep if I tell you that back in my youth I learned to play poker. Art Newburn held some delusions that he was a poker player. I won't go into the sad details but convinced him otherwise."[7]

up acting like a coward when he runs from a wounded lion. But maybe he is just being smart.

The professional hunter, Robert Wilson, is a handsome, strong man. Macomber's wife makes fun of her cowardly husband to Wilson, and she even offers herself romantically to Wilson that night. The whole safari is uncomfortable because of the cowardice of Francis Macomber, the embarrassment of his wife, and the rugged good looks of Wilson. Wilson also breaks his code as a hunter when he allows Mr. Macomber to chase game while riding in the car. Remember that it is terrible for the code to be broken, so Hemingway is letting the readers know that Wilson might not be a good person if he lets his codes be broken so easily.

To make up for his cowardly fleeing, Francis Macomber goes in the bush to kill a wounded bull buffalo, which he thought he did. After that earlier embarrassing moment, he now feels brave. "As the car moved slowly across the open space toward the island of bushy trees that ran in a tongue of foliage along a dry water course that cut the open swale, Macomber felt his heart pounding and his mouth was dry again, but it was excitement, not fear."[8]

The gun bearer says the bull buffalo is dead, but then it comes charging out of the bush. Wilson and Macomber take a few shots at the furious beast. Mrs. Macomber, who sees the incident from a distance, takes a shot, too. Her shot does not hit the buffalo. It hits and kills her husband.

The question readers ask themselves is this: Did Margot Macomber aim to kill the buffalo or her husband? If she did intend to shoot her husband, did she do it because he was a coward or because she was afraid of his new courage? Did she shoot at the charging bull buffalo to save her husband or Wilson? Maybe she is braver than her husband is. Maybe she wanted to save Wilson in order to further a relationship with him. Maybe she is a murderer.

On the other hand, perhaps she intended to shoot Robert Wilson. If so, did she do it because she wanted to start a fresh relationship with her husband? After all, Wilson did duck right before Mrs. Macomber's shot. She also made the shot from the car, something she earlier noted was unfair and wrong.

The last page of the story reveals what Wilson and Mrs. Macomber say they believe. Is what they say the truth? In order to answer this question, we have to consider how Mrs. Macomber felt about her husband. Compared to the great hunter Wilson, Francis Macomber seems like a weak man. Although they have been married for eleven years, at the beginning of the story Margot Macomber looks at both her husband and Wilson "as though she had never seen them before."[9]

Since it is as if she has never seen them before, we can forget the history Francis and Margot Macomber have. Now we can compare Robert Wilson to Francis Macomber. Wilson had "extremely cold blue eyes with faint white wrinkles at the corners that grooved merrily when he smiled." He has large shotgun shells in his belt, and Mrs. Macomber notices "his big brown hands, his old slacks, his very dirty boots."[10] Wilson is a real man, not just someone who wears manly clothes and pretends to be a real man.

Francis is described as being "very well built if you did not mind that length of bone, dark, his hair cropped like an oarsman, rather thin-lipped, and was considered handsome. He was dressed in the same sort of safari clothes that Wilson wore except that his were new […] and he had just shown himself, very publicly, to be a coward."[11] Macomber dresses like a real man, but his manliness does not seem to go beyond his clothing. His wife makes it clear she respects real men, and she works to make her husband seem even weaker. Hemingway writes that women like Margot Macomber are "predatory."[12] This means that they live by destroying others. In this sense, Mrs. Macomber and Robert Wilson are the same; they are both predators. Mrs. Macomber lives by destroying her husband, and Wilson lives by destroying wild animals.

Macomber's Codes

One aspect of "The Short Happy Life of Francis Macomber" is codes and code breaking. The story depicts the strict rules of big game hunting and the code of the bush. Wilson breaks a few rules: He allows game chasing from the car and he lashes the natives instead of making them pay fines. Wilson thinks

Hemingway on his boat the *Pilar*, fishing the waters off Cuba.

that his standards (his code) could change if his clients had different standards:

> Their standards were his standards as long as they were hiring him.

> They were his standards in all except the shooting. He had his own standards about the killing and they could live up to them or get someone else to hunt them. He knew, too, that they all respected him for this.[13]

So maybe Robert Wilson does have a code that he does not break. There are instances in Hemingway's fiction where a person's code and the code of law conflict. There are times when a character breaks a law because he has to in order to keep from breaking his own code. Wilson does not care about stealing another man's wife or allowing Macomber to chase game in a car. He does not break his code about not allowing an animal to suffer more than it has to, and he never talks about other people who have hired him because he is a professional hunter.

Hemingway based "The Short Happy Life of Francis Macomber" on people he met on his hunting expeditions in Africa, although the shooting of Francis Macomber never happened in real life. Hemingway seemed to have a mind built for writing. He would see and experience something, then he would think about it and the possible connections and outcomes. Finally, he would put his ideas into words. His stories are based on reality, but they are still fiction.

Again to War

Ernest Hemingway bought a fine fishing boat he named the *Pilar* to dock at his Key West home. Off the coast of Key West, he once caught a 514-pound (233 kg) tuna. This, too, he would later write about. He also met a woman from St. Louis named Martha Gellhorn. She was a journalist, and she began to spend more and more time with Ernest and Pauline.

Hemingway was thirty-eight years old, and he wanted some excitement. He got news that his favorite places in Northern Spain were being overtaken in a civil war. The Spanish Civil War began in July 1936. The Nationalists, with help from Nazi Germany and fascist Italy, were battling the Loyalists. Hemingway was strongly against Nazism and fascism, and he took an interest in the Loyalist side. He traveled to Spain in March of 1937. Year ago he had volunteered to be in the action of World War I mainly because it seemed exciting. Now he went to Spain as a journalist because he did not want to see the country he had come to love taken over by people with bad ideas.

Throughout his entire life, Ernest Hemingway read almost constantly. What he read and what he experienced in Spain would provide material for his next huge success. He went to Spain to join his friend John dos Passos and Dutch filmmaker Joris Ivens to make a film about conditions in Spain (*The Spanish Earth*) as well as write newspaper articles. He returned to America to help raise money for ambulances in Spain to help the wounded soldiers. Martha Gellhorn also went to Spain, and she and Ernest sadly watched Loyalist forces being overtaken. Pauline, back in Paris, knew she was losing Ernest to Martha. They eventually divorced in December 1939.

In February 1939, Hemingway made a trip to Cuba and began writing another novel. Within three weeks, he had written 15,000 words.[14] He and Martha began renting a large but run-down house near Havana. Hemingway eventually bought the house as a Christmas gift to himself in 1940. This house, called Finca Vigia (Spanish for "lookout farm"), would be the place where Hemingway would do some of his finest writing.

He finished the new novel in August, and he thought it was the best book he had yet written. He titled it *For Whom the Bell Tolls*.

"No Man Is an Island"

For Whom the Bell Tolls is an interesting and difficult book. It balances war with romantic love and shows how war affects real people. The title of the novel comes from a book by John Donne, an English poet who lived four hundred years ago. In his book titled *Devotions Upon Emergent Occasions*, Donne writes:

> No man is an Iland, intire of it selfe; every man is a peece of the Continent, a part of the maine [...] any man's death diminishes me, because I am involved in Mankinde; And therefore never send to know for whom the bell tolls; It tolls for thee.[15]

Donne means that all people are connected, and one person cannot live completely alone. In the old days, church bells would ring when a person was buried. Donne felt his connection to other people so strongly that he did not need to know for whom the bell was ringing. When anyone died, he felt a piece of himself die. All people are connected, and we shouldn't think that we are separated from the rest of the world.

This is how Robert Jordan, the hero of *For Whom the Bell Tolls* feels, too. Jordan is an American fighting on the Loyalist side on the Spanish Civil War. He is assigned to stay with unofficial fighters living in a cave on a hillside. His goal is to blow up an important bridge. The story of the 471-page novel

Hemingway in Spain as a correspondent during the Spanish Civil War.

takes place over only seventy hours, but what happens during that time changes Jordan forever.

Jordan falls in love with a young Spanish woman named Maria. Almost from the start, she loves him, too. Maria was abused by the people the Loyalists are fighting. When they are together, Jordan and Maria try to forget about the war, but it is impossible. Along with a few other soldiers, a woman named Pilar and her husband Pablo live in the cave. Jordan thinks Pablo is a drunk, stupid man, but Pilar tells Jordan a story of how Pablo showed his bravery in battle. The story is intense and unforgettable. Pilar trembles when thinking of the story because it seems that Pablo finds pleasure in killing. The story is brutal. It also shows that Pablo is smart in a certain way, and Jordan is not sure how to handle him.

Hemingway includes this story to show how war is more than dots on a chart or numbers of casualties. War means children losing their parents, painful injuries, and people doing things they may later regret.

A Life in Three Days

As Robert Jordan tries to carry out his mission, his love for Maria and the foolishness of Pablo and other hill fighters almost ruin his plans. Compare the first and last sentences of *For Whom the Bell Tolls*. First sentence: "He lay flat on the brown, pine-needled floor of the forest, his chin on his folded arms, and high overhead the wind blew in the tops of the pine trees." Last sentence: "He could feel his heart beating against the pine needle floor of the forest."

The setting is the same. However, a great deal has happened to Jordan and the other characters in the novel. By making the ending so much like the beginning, Hemingway makes the story seem like a circle. It seems as though this thing has happened before and that it will happen again. This is another clever trick Hemingway uses. He wrote this novel so readers would really care what happens to Jordan and Maria, but he also wrote it to be more open. The story is about Jordan and Maria, but it could be about people in other wars in other parts of the world at other times in history.

It is also interesting to note that, at the beginning and ending of the novel, Jordan is by himself. He is in nature, but there are no other people with him.

Cutting Dialogue

Real-life history plays an important role in *For Whom the Bell Tolls*. Hemingway writes about the actual Spanish Civil War, but he makes up characters. Some generals and soldiers in the novel are based on real people, but other characters are created from his imagination. Again, the characters he creates show how war is much more than maps and numbers. War can tear apart families and kill good people.

The first person Robert Jordan meets by the gypsy cave is an old man named Anselmo. Although he admits he has killed enemy soldiers in battle, Anselmo thinks killing a person is very bad. When Jordan asks Anselmo if he has ever killed anyone, Anselmo answers, "Yes. Several times. But not with pleasure. To me it is a sin to kill a man. Even the Fascists whom we must kill. […] I am against the killing of men."[16] Anselmo has a code.

Late in the book, Anselmo is killed, and Jordan feels very bad about his death, but it is partially Pablo's fault. Even in the confusion and noise of battle, Jordan feels sadness at Anselmo's death. Jordan knows that he, himself, is part of this terrible war even though he hates it. The mission of blowing up the bridge is very important to Jordan, but the lives of Maria and the others on the hillside become very important as well. Like other code heroes, Jordan is more concerned with the safety of others than with his own. In the intense, dramatic conclusion of the novel, Jordan thinks, "Each one does what he can. You can do nothing for yourself but perhaps you can do something for another."[17] This is another time when codes might cause conflict. Sometimes codes have to be changed, but that is a big decision that must be considered carefully.

The dialogue in *For Whom the Bell Tolls* confuses many readers because it has many old-fashioned words like "thee" and "whom." For example, the gypsy Anselmo says to Pablo, "Until now thou hadst horses thou wert with us."[18] In more modern English, Anselmo means, "Until you had horses you were with us." Hemingway wrote this way for two reasons. First, the characters would have spoken Spanish. The actual translations of many Spanish words are these old sounding words. In Spanish, there are formal ways to refer to someone you do not know very well and informal ways to refer to a close friend. These characters are using the first, more formal way, and that is translated into English as "thee," "thou," and so on.

The second reason for this style of writing is to give the book a classic sound. Hemingway uses the old style of the John Donne quote ("It tolls for thee") throughout the entire book. Bridging the formal sounding words to the down-to-earth parts helps the reader understand the bigger picture while feeling the personal effects of the civil war. The struggle Pilar, Pablo, Maria, and the others are facing is a classic struggle of individuals against aggressive political leaders.

Throughout the novel, Robert Jordan is torn between his duty and his love for Maria. When he is alone with Maria, Jordan tries as hard as he can not to think about the war. But

TIME IN *FOR WHOM THE BELL TOLLS*

In his book *Hemingway, Style, and the Art of Emotion*, David Wyatt argues that the focus of *For Whom the Bell Tolls* is time. Jordan and Maria are together for only seventy hours. "None of Hemingway's books spends so much time talking about 'time,' and none attempts as many experiments with how to fill rather than to kill it," Wyatt writes.[19] There is significance to how long the characters have been fighting for the cause. Jordan wonders how long Pablo can fight off the fascists. The difference in age between Jordan and Anselmo is an important aspect of their friendship. And, of course, the bridge must be blown at a certain time. Time is indeed an important part of this novel. As you read it, think about how time is important in the story of Robert Jordan.

when he is busy preparing to blow up the bridge, Jordan forces himself not to think about Maria. After Jordan shoots an enemy scout, he feels Maria next to him. Hemingway writes, "She had no place in his life now."[20]

Despite their efforts, the Loyalists in the Spanish Civil War were overpowered. *For Whom the Bell Tolls* ends with Jordan in a very interesting position. It is certainly not the kind of ending found in most novels before Hemingway's time. Readers have to figure out for themselves if there will be a satisfactory ending. Maybe life is futile, and the only way to happiness is to try to be a good person and not expect fair treatment.

It is important to keep in mind that *For Whom the Bell Tolls* is a mature book. Hemingway meant for it to be read by adults, and it has a few adult themes. It is also a long book. Hemingway wrote the novel when he was forty years old, and he had experienced much in those forty years. Much of the language and many scenes in the book make it clear that this is not a romantic book.

The brilliance of *For Whom the Bell Tolls* is that it seems like more than just a story about war and love between two people. It is a story about how people treat each other and what life is about. Jordan does not have to risk his life fighting in Spain but he does it to help people in need. He eventually does much, much more than his duty calls for. He realizes that people are connected; it does not matter where people are from or how they live, as long as they try to be good.

Jordan thinks, "I suppose it is possible to live as full a life in seventy hours as in seventy years; granted that your life has been full up to the time that the seventy hours start and that you have reached a certain age."[21] After this sentence, he thinks about what love means. Then he thinks about how terrible war is. The way the novel shifts from dialogue to Jordan's thoughts confuses some readers because Jordan is not the teller of the story but a character in it. However, many readers appreciate being able to see the scenes and also see into Jordan's thoughts.

For Whom the Bell Tolls was selected to receive the Pulitzer Prize for Fiction in 1941. The Pulitzer Prize is a very important award for the best work of the year. It has been given every year since 1918. The head of the Pulitzer board, however, said the novel could not win the prize because it had a few scenes he considered profane, and he vetoed the selection of Hemingway's book.[22] There was no Pulitzer Prize for Fiction for 1941.

"I Went Out Too Far": The Old Man and the Sea

By 1941, World War II was a terrible reality in Europe. Hemingway saw the war as an extension of the Spanish Civil War, and being on the losing side of that conflict left a bitter taste in his mouth. He hated war, but he also hated forces who try to make people do what they don't want to do. Martha Hemingway, a journalist, longed for adventure, and set out to Europe to write about the war. Her husband stayed in Cuba, spending his days fishing. It angered Martha that Ernest was not more interested in the largest war in history, and their marriage was stressed. When Hemingway eventually went to London to meet up with his wife, he also met a journalist named Mary Welsh. She was very pretty, and Hemingway was immediately attracted to her.

One interesting episode in Hemingway's time in Cuba concerns his hunt for German submarines while aboard the *Pilar* in the waters around Cuba. In 1942 and 1943, he would take out his boat, outfitted with weapons to blow up a submarine or battle with German marines, and patrol for submarines. The FBI knew of his patrols and somewhat encouraged him, although he did not conduct these patrols as the FBI would have liked. Hemingway seemed more eager to fight German submarines himself than report them to the US government.

Hemingway stands outside Finca Vigía ("Lookout Farm"), his home outside Havana, Cuba.

He had a couple of possible sightings, but not much came from his patrols other than an interesting FBI file.

Hemingway managed to be present as a journalist at the historical Allied landing at Omaha Beach on the coast of England on D-Day (June 6, 1944). He did this less than two weeks after being in a serious car accident. Although he was only supposed to observe and write about war events for *Collier's* magazine, Hemingway saw some real battle action. He bragged about his adventures to Mary Welsh, with whom he eventually fell in love. He divorced Martha right before Christmas 1945, and he married Mary Welsh, his fourth wife, the following March.

Across the River and Into the Trees

In 1949, Hemingway traveled from his house in Cuba to the place in Italy where he had been seriously injured over thirty years earlier. This was a moving visit for him, and back in Cuba he wrote about how he felt as an older man returning to the spot where he became a man. He titled this new novel *Across the River and into the Trees*, and it was published in September 1950. The novel is about a fifty-year-old military colonel who returns to Venice to spend time with a nineteen-year-old girl he has loved for some time. This time, combat is not the featured event, as it had been in *For Whom the Bell Tolls*.

Across the River and into the Trees was not well received by critics, but Hemingway liked it. As in "A Clean, Well-Lighted Place," this novel centers on an older man whose dignity is still intact. His rough life is catching up to him, and he realizes he is not the strong man he once was. However, Colonel Cantwell is proud of his military service, and he does not care what people might think about him dating a girl so much younger than he is.

Colonel Cantwell was a military hero much like the real-life Andrew Jackson. General Jackson is known for his bravery in the Battle of New Orleans. He also served two terms as president of the United States. In *Across the River and into the Trees*, Hemingway writes that Jackson's dying words were that he and his soldiers should go "across the river and into the trees" to rest. These are some of Colonel Cantwell's dying words, too. The comparison between Jackson and Cantwell is another example of how Hemingway's knowledge of history entered his writing.

After Christmas 1950, Hemingway began writing the story of a Cuban fisherman, and the story was finished by the end of February 1951. It was considered too short to publish as a novel by itself, so *Life* magazine published it in a special edition titled *The Old Man and the Sea*, and it was an immediate, huge hit.

The Influence of Tolstoy

The Old Man and the Sea is another example of Hemingway's iceberg theory. The basic story is simple: an old fisherman goes a long time without catching any fish. Then he catches a large marlin far out at sea by himself and struggles to bring it in for days. Ultimately, sharks eat the huge fish as he hauls it back to port. His friend, a boy named Manolin, helps him back to his tiny shack. There is much more to this story, however. Santiago, the fisherman, and his catch are an allegory of a bigger story.

An allegory is a simple story with deeper meanings. A person, object, or event can have more than one meaning. For example, some see the back-and-forth between Santiago and the marlin as representing the fight between man and nature. Others see Santiago and his struggle with the huge

allegory

A writing device in which a person, object, or event has a deeper meaning than what is seen on the surface.

fish to be about how people can suffer disappointments and still persevere. The fish could represent anything that a person struggles for.

Sometimes students are faced with two options on a test in school. They can study hard and hope they get a good score, or they can not study at all and cheat. The cheaters might end up with a higher score on the test, but those who studied can feel better about themselves. Santiago is like those who studied for the test. While the younger fishermen make fun of him, Santiago does not let himself get angry. In addition, he loves Manolin like a son, but never forgets that the boy has his own parents.

About Santiago, Hemingway writes, "He was too simple to wonder when he had attained humility. But he knew he had attained it and he knew it was not disgraceful and it carried no loss of true pride."[1] This means that Santiago knew he was humble, but he knew it was real and not fake humility. He thinks that being honest and true to what you believe is what makes a man. Although Manolin is young, Santiago tells him "You are already a man."[2] He says this because Manolin helps him, and he seems not to focus only on himself.

Quite often, people do eventually get what they want, but it is not exactly as good as they thought it would be. All humans end up dying; it is how one lives that makes the difference. This idea appears in a short story titled "The Death of Ivan Ilyich" by Leo Tolstoy. Hemingway admired the writings of Tolstoy, even though Tolstoy wrote about fifty years before Hemingway was born. How well a writer writes is more important than when he or she writes. Again, Hemingway's reading and ability to observe life were the things that helped him become a famous writer.

Ernest Hemingway did not use the phrase the Lost Generation to refer to himself because he felt he was writing about more than how one generation lived. People of all generations feel lost at some point. Similarly, *The Old Man and the Sea* is a story about anyone in any time. It is a short book, but its meaning runs long.

"No Hay Derecho"

Ernest Hemingway wrote about all kinds of people, from military generals to killers. These characters might be good or bad, but the one trait that is always important in Hemingway's fiction is dignity, the quality of being worthy of respect. Having no dignity is terrible, he believed, and it is also terrible when someone's dignity is disrespected. In Spanish, *derecho* means "right," as in the direction, but it also means "right" as in something that you have the authority to do.

In a short story called "The Butterfly and the Tank," a man comes into a bar in Spain crowded with soldiers and shoots an experienced waiter with a water gun (called a "flit gun" in the story). Hemingway writes:

> Everybody laughed except the waiter who was carrying a tray full of drinks at the time. He was indignant.
>
> "No hay derecho," the waiter said. This means, "You have no right to do that," and this is the simplest and strongest protest in Spain.
>
> [The man shoots another waiter with his water gun.]
>
> "No hay derecho," he said with dignity.
>
> [The man shoots another waiter with his water gun.]

> "No hay derecho," he said. This time it was no protest. It was an indictment and I saw three men in uniform start from a table for the flit gun man and the next thing all four of them were going out the revolving door in a rush and you heard a smack when someone hit the flit gun man on the mouth.[3]

Doing something you have no right to do is a very bad thing in this Spanish bar, as it is a bad thing in *The Old Man and the Sea*. The flit gun man is not just hit in the mouth but also shot and killed. He did not have a respectable code. The flit gun man did something that was unfair, and he suffered the ultimate price for it. Santiago does what is right and dignified, and he feels good about himself for it.

This idea of right and wrong appears in much of Hemingway's writing. A character does not have respect for a general just because he is a general. A character respects only those people who are honest and fair. These people who are respected might be generals or they might be streetwalkers (as in "The Light of the World") or weak old men (as in "Old Man at the Bridge"). Of course, different people have different ideas of right and wrong. To Hemingway, dignity meant doing what you think is right. Also, he believed people should not work to hurt those they think do wrong unless they are really hurting someone.

About *The Old Man and the Sea*, the American writer William Faulkner wrote:

> Time may show it to be the best single piece of any of us. I mean his and my contemporaries. This time, he discovered God, a Creator. Until now, his men and women had made themselves, shaped themselves out of their own clay; their victories and defeats were at the hands of each other, just to prove to themselves or

one another how tough they could be. But this time, he wrote about pity; about something somewhere that made them all: the old man who had to catch the fish and then lose it, the fish that had to be caught and then lost, the sharks which had to rob the old man of his fish; made them all and loved them all and pitied them all. It's all right. Praise God that whatever made and loves and pities Hemingway and me kept him from touching it any further.[4]

Faulkner claims that the pity Hemingway plays with in *The Sun Also Rises* is mastered in *The Old Man and the Sea*. The reader feels pity for Santiago because he worked so long catching the fish only to bring back the fish's skeleton. However, Santiago does not feel pity for himself.

When the first group of sharks start tearing up his record-setting marlin, Santiago talks to himself:

It was too good to last, he thought. I wish it had been a dream now and that I had never hooked the fish and was alone in bed on the newspapers.

"But man is not made for defeat," he said. "A man can be destroyed but not defeated."[5]

By bringing back a marlin that is little more than a skeleton, he is destroyed. After struggling with the huge fish for two days, he has hardly any meat to sell. He is not defeated, however, because he knows he fought a good fight, and he won. He was there, out at sea, and he saw the huge, beautiful marlin he caught. In fact, Santiago feels pity for the marlin. He does not give in to feeling sorry for himself. That is his dignity. After the second bunch of sharks come and eat the marlin, Santiago says, "I wish it were a dream and that I had never hooked him. I'm sorry about it, fish. It makes every-

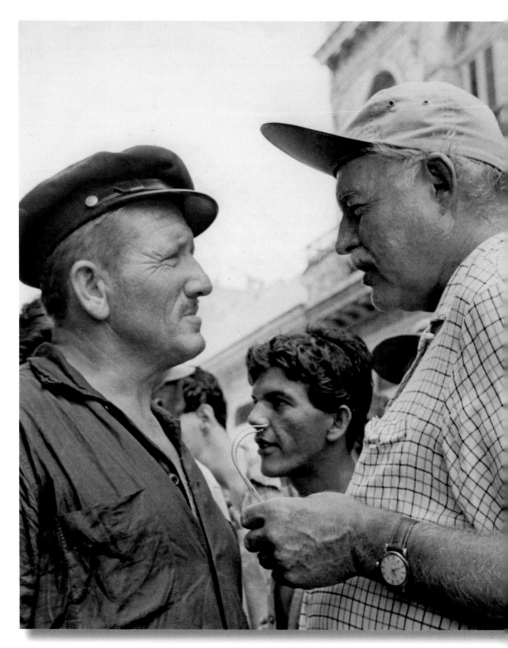

Hemingway talks with actor Spencer Tracy on the set of the 1958 film version of *The Old Man and the Sea*. The men became friends and shared many stories.

thing wrong."[6] If Santiago had felt pity for himself, it would have been all wrong. In Faulkner's words, "It's all right" because feeling sorry for oneself means being defeated. Santiago is not defeated.

The simple story of Santiago losing his fish is an allegory of man suffering defeat. Although some other fishermen laugh at Santiago for having such bad luck fishing, Santiago remains dignified. He does not talk meanly to those fishermen; he merely hopes he will catch a fish the next day. He is proud at how perfect he keeps his fishing lines, and he has certain ways of doing things. He has dignity.

Santiago loves the ocean and treats nature like people:

> He was very fond of flying fish as they were his principal friends on the ocean. He was sorry for the birds, especially the small delicate dark terns that were always flying and looking and almost never finding, and he thought, the birds have a harder life than we do except for the robber birds and the heavy strong ones. Why did they make birds so delicate and fine as those sea swallows when the ocean can be so cruel?[7]

This is an example of irony in nature. Santiago wonders how the sea can be so beautiful and kind and also so cruel and wicked. He thinks it is because that is the sea's nature, and she (the sea) cannot help it.

Santiago, Ahab, and Jesus

There are several examples of allusions in *The Old Man and the Sea*. One such example can be found in the parallel between this novel and the classic *Moby Dick*. In *The Old Man and the Sea*, an old sailor risks everything to pursue a mysterious sea creature, a storyline similar to that of *Moby Dick*. *The Old Man and the Sea* was published almost exactly

allusion
A writing device in which a scene, person, or event in one book or story refers to something else.

one hundred years after *Moby Dick*. One could say the basic storyline of *The Old Man and the Sea* is an allusion to *Moby Dick*.

Another example of allusion in the novel is biblical. Santiago makes his way back to the harbor in the darkness, and there is no one to help him dock his boat. He ties his boat to a rock, removes the mast, and begins to carry it on his shoulder back to his shack. As he carries the mast up the hill, he stumbles and has to rest. He puts the mast back on his shoulder and tries to walk on. Santiago carrying the mast on his shoulder can be seen as an allusion to the scene in the New Testament of the Bible where Jesus carries the cross upon which he is to be crucified. In the Bible, Jesus falls three times on the way to his crucifixion. It can be argued that Hemingway is comparing Santiago with Jesus Christ. Both men suffered but were not totally defeated. Both men were fishermen. And both men were surrounded by people who did not believe in them.

Hemingway also invokes Jesus's plight in the scene when Santiago sees more sharks coming to attack his marlin: "'Ay,'" he said aloud. There is no translation for this word and perhaps it is just a noise such as a man might make, involuntarily, feeling the nail go through his hands and into the wood."[8]

This description could allude to Jesus, and the wood could be the cross he was crucified on. A reader must be careful not to think that Hemingway definitely wrote *The Old Man and the Sea* to be a Christian allegory because other readers might find a different allegory. We don't know for certain what Hemingway meant because he did not let anyone know.

MOBY DICK

Moby Dick (1851) is a novel by Herman Melville centering on the character Captain Ahab and his quest to destroy the great, white whale, Moby Dick. On the surface, the novel brilliantly captures the exciting and dramatic life aboard a nineteenth-century whaling ship. On another level, however, *Moby Dick* is a deep allegory, with the whale symbolizing the mysterious forces of the universe, and Captain Ahab representing the human struggle to understand and conquer those forces. In the classic novel, Captain Ahab seems to both hate and admire the whale that is so difficult to capture. We see this in *The Old Man and the Sea*, too, although Santiago seems to respect the huge fish more than hate it.

When thinking about what symbols in literature mean, it is important to provide evidence to support your interpretation. The many different interpretations of literature are part of what makes good writing so interesting.

Both Jesus and Santiago were destroyed but not defeated. After so many painful injuries, lost loves, and other struggles, Hemingway himself must have felt that he was slowly being destroyed through his later years. The last years of Ernest Hemingway's life slowly destroyed this great writer, and his final destruction came from within.

THE SUN SETS: LIFE TAKES ITS TOLL

The journey to becoming America's most famous writer was not without its rough spots. Along the way, Ernest Hemingway had made many enemies, wasted much money, and almost wore himself out. He had built a very distinctive image for himself and his writing, and many people are still unsure where Hemingway ends and his characters begin. There are pieces of him and his acquaintances throughout his writing. Hemingway played as hard as he worked, and this became harder to do as he aged. His many injuries were bothering him more and more, and the public wanted better and better writing from him. He was no longer a teenage cub reporter for the *Kansas City Star*. Still, he enjoyed parties with other writers, long meals with his friends, and longer days fishing aboard the *Pilar*.

In 1953, Ernest and Mary Hemingway went on another African safari to celebrate Ernest's recent writing successes. He was making a lot of money by having his books made into movies, and *The Old Man and the Sea* was still selling like crazy. In fact, that book won him the Pulitzer Prize for 1952. In Africa, Hemingway hunted big game and enjoyed the fresh air. But then the Hemingways were in two airplane accidents. Word got out, and some newspapers published the news that Ernest Hemingway and his wife had been killed in a plane wreck.

Hemingway with his fourth wife, Mary, in the 1950s. They married in Cuba, and Mary has a cameo role in the film *The Old Man and the Sea.*

Ernest and Mary Hemingway survived both crashes, but Ernest was badly wounded. He used his head as a battering ram to bust open the jammed door of the burning airplane. Surviving two airplane crashes in Africa helped build his image as an indestructible superman, but his head was badly injured, and he suffered injuries to his liver, spine, and arms. He also suffered burns. Hemingway tried to hide the pain his injuries caused him, but he moved much slower. He was in pain much of the time. The plane wrecks slowed his thinking and writing, and that depressed him.

Winning the Nobel Prize

Hemingway's spirits were lifted when he was awarded the Nobel Prize for Literature in 1954. He was too ill to go to the awards ceremony, but he wrote a speech that someone else read. In his speech, Hemingway wrote, "A writer should write what he has to say and not speak it."[1] In other words, good writing is not like listening to a storyteller. Good writing should allow the reader to hear the story in his or her own voice. The author's voice should be silent. Many other authors and poets (notably T. S. Eliot) agreed with this idea—that

HEMINGWAY AND TWAIN

Hemingway was not the only famous writer to have his death falsely reported. The beloved American writer Mark Twain also had the news of his death published before he actually died. Hemingway greatly admired Twain, and in his 1935 book *Green Hills of Africa*, he wrote, "All Modern American literature comes from one book by Mark Twain called *Huckleberry Finn*."[2] There are many similarities between the lives and writing of Mark Twain and Ernest Hemingway.

good writing lets readers forget about the writer and lose themselves in the actual story.

In his acceptance speech, Hemingway also wrote that writing is a lonely business. A writer has to do a lot of thinking, and a writer has to work alone. The reward of completing a complicated chapter or describing a certain event in the best words is hard to communicate to someone else, so many of the rewards of being a writer are for the writer only. It is hard to share that feeling of accomplishment.

Hemingway grew sicker and sicker throughout the late 1950s. Years of heavy alcohol drinking and numerous accidents had weakened his body, but he tried to continue writing. It also seemed that he had difficulties thinking, but he began rewriting a long novel he had started several years earlier.

The Hemingways eventually bought a house in Ketchum, Idaho. Hemingway thought Ketchum would be a good place to relax, write, and enjoy nature. In the summer of 1959, Ernest and Mary Hemingway sailed to Spain one last time. Some scholars call this "the dangerous summer" for several reasons: Some of Hemingway's bullfighter friends were severely injured, Hemingway worked and partied to exhaustion, and his depression deepened. Hemingway's marriage also grew strained, and he was having financial difficulties.

But Hemingway felt the need to continue writing. He did not want the public to think he was washed up as a writer. He had always demanded the best of himself, and he did not want to let himself or his readers down. Writing had become a part of his life; he could not survive without it.

His Last Days

By 1960, Ernest Hemingway's health was quite bad. In addition to his physical injuries and complaints, his mind seems to have been slipping. He began to think the FBI and other officials were spying on him. He was admitted to the hospital twice for psychiatric treatment, but he was allowed to return to his Ketchum, Idaho, house with his wife, Mary.

At the hospital, Hemingway underwent electroshock therapy. This is a medical treatment in which an electric current is passed into the patient's brain. It is usually used when other treatments have failed. This all but destroyed his ability to write. For a man whose life was shaped by his writing, this must have been a terrible time. Occasionally, Hemingway seemed almost like his old self, but most of the time he was

Mary and a bearded Ernest Hemingway at a bullfight in 1959.

paranoid and depressed. Mary did what she could to help him feel better, but Ernest had always been an independent man.

He thought about suicide, and his friends and his wife caught him more than once holding a gun as if he were going to shoot himself. By the middle of 1961, Hemingway was certainly not his old self. He could not concentrate, and he was terribly upset that he could no longer think clearly enough to write.

Ending His Life

Early on the Sunday morning of July 2, 1961, Ernest Hemingway woke up before Mary. He loaded one of his favorite shotguns, and he killed himself. He was buried in Ketchum, Idaho. Ernest Hemingway's three sons and three of his four sisters attended the funeral.

In his will, Hemingway instructed that his personal letters be destroyed, and most of them were. Many letters and drafts of stories survived, however, and are held in a few libraries across America. Correspondence stored in his Cuba home was recently released to American researchers, who are carefully cataloging the letters.

The same hunger for adventure and desire to write that fueled Ernest Hemingway for so many years were part of his eventual self-destruction.

THE HEMINGWAY LEGACY: ERNEST HEMINGWAY AND HIS WORK TODAY

Hemingway wanted his writing output to speak for him after his death and not details and tales about his life. Even though he asked his wife Mary to burn all his letters and notes when he died, several books by Hemingway were published after his death: *A Moveable Feast* (published in 1964), *Islands in the Stream* (1970), *Hemingway's Selected Letters 1917–1961* (1981), *The Garden of Eden* (1986), and *True at First Light* (1999). These books were not finished by Hemingway but were put together by either family members or editors. Most critics do not find these books to be as well-written as his earlier ones, but Hemingway's characteristic style carried through to these later works.

Scholars, students, and researchers continue to study Hemingway's writing style and to enjoy his writing. Hemingway was an exceptional person. He had adventures most people can only imagine, but he created stories and characters we can all enjoy. From his earliest poems to his newspaper articles to his posthumous novels, his writing is real. It is not about a romanticized or ideal world but the real world. His writing is as sacred as it is profane, as joyful as it is depressing.

Hemingway Changed American Literature

The joy in Hemingway's writing may be found in his basic enjoyment of life. The feel of icy cold water in a trout stream,

Hemingway in 1959, showing his age but still enjoying sailing.

the taste of pasta *asciutta* on the battlefield, the sight of lions on the beach in Africa, the sound of silk worms eating mulberry leaves—they are all signs of life. Things are not always good, and sometimes bad things happen to good people. Still, we live to stay true to our code and try to help others. This is the message in Hemingway's writing.

Hemingway believed that writing is a lonely business, but he also believed that people couldn't live without other people. Nick Adams goes to the Big Two-Hearted River to be alone, but he remembers his friend Hopkins, with whom he used to camp. Frederic Henry and Catherine Barkley, and Robert Jordan and Maria are couples that loved each other so much that they felt as though they were one person. Jordan says to Maria, "You are also me now. . . . Thou art me too now."[1]

The code hero never gives up, and Ernest Hemingway gave up only once—that Sunday morning in 1961.

Hemingway forever changed American literature. The iceberg that is Ernest Hemingway and his writing is still there for us to explore. Hemingway began writing in a style that is quite common now. Not all endings have to be happy ones where all problems are solved; not all heroes have to be perfect in every way; not all good people are rewarded; and not all bad people are punished.

How He Wrote

Hemingway wrote about characters who were not really connected with any bigger group. The characters with dignity are usually not connected with a political party or even a particular country. This idea was rather new in literature, and it was a major idea in modernism.

As populations grew and the world became more and more busy, the individual seemed lost. Many writers before

Hemingway looked at groups of people—nationalities, social groups, and armies. Hemingway wrote about one person in an army or one man on the sea. Not just that, Hemingway wrote about what that one person thinks and what it is like when the battle is over or the hero returns home with the mere skeleton of a big catch.

In *A Moveable Feast*, Hemingway wrote about how he did his actual writing when he lived in Paris:

> I always worked until I had something done and I always stopped when I knew what was going to happen next. That way I could be sure of going on the next day. But sometimes when I was starting a new story and I could not get it going, I would sit in front of the fire and squeeze the peel of the little oranges into the edge of the flame and watch the sputter of blue that they made. I would stand and look over the roofs of Paris and think, "Do not worry. You have always written before and you will write now. All you have to do is write one true sentence. Write the truest sentence that you know."[2]

He wrote about what he thought was true and real. This was not always an easy assignment for Hemingway, and he felt extremely happy after he had written.

In that same book he writes, "There is never any ending to Paris and the memory of each person who has lived in it differs from that of any other."[3]

Write One True Sentence

Hemingway's idea of one true sentence runs along the same lines as those memories of Paris. What one person believes is true might not work for another person. Hemingway wrote in a very factual manner so that readers can "fill in" color and extra detail as they want. It does not matter if the year is 1926 or 2026; his writing will still have meaning for readers who put forth the effort to read carefully and think about what they have read. Even though Hemingway is considered to be part of the Lost Generation, his writing is timeless.

Hemingway Today

Ernest Hemingway's residences in Oak Park, Illinois; Paris, France; Key West, Florida; outside Havana, Cuba; Ketchum, Idaho; and other places are tourist destinations now. They have been preserved to give visitors the feeling that Hemingway is alive, just upstairs preparing for another writing session. Maybe he is seated at his desk, pondering one true sentence to begin a new novel. Maybe he is on the veranda, sipping wine in celebration of another twelve-page day.

Although Hemingway is gone, his personality and writing are still with us. His writing style changed American literature forever. The short declarative sentence, the principle of the iceberg, and Hemingway's use of pity and irony are the foundation upon which today's fiction is built.

Hemingway Lives On...

...in Key West: Every year in July, to celebrate Hemingway's birthday, a Hemingway Days festival is thrown in Key West, Florida. Over 120 men compete in an Ernest Hemingway look-alike contest, there is a 5K (3.1 mile) race and a fishing tournament, and the look-alike contestants ride fake bulls down Whitehead Street, where Hemingway and his wife Pauline lived. This tradition continues today.

...in published works: Even now, well over 115 years after his death, dozens of books are published every year on Hemingway's life and work. All of his surviving letters are being written as a series of books (*The Letters of Ernest*

ONE TRUE SENTENCE?

Here are the first sentences of a few of Hemingway's works. Think about them. To the author, they are true sentences. Do these sentences make you want to read on? Can you write sentences that, to you, are true?

In Our Time: Everybody was drunk.

The Sun Also Rises: Robert Cohn was once middleweight boxing champion of Princeton.

A Farewell to Arms: In the late summer of that year we lived in a house in a village that looked across the river and the plain to the mountains.

For Whom the Bell Tolls: He lay flat on the brown, pine-needled floor of the forest, his chin on his folded arms, and high overhead the wind blew in the tops of the pine trees.

The Old Man and the Sea: He was an old man who fished alone in a skiff in the Gulf Stream and he had gone eighty-four days now without taking a fish.

A Moveable Feast: Then there was the bad weather.

The Green Hills of Africa: We were sitting in the blind that Wanderobo hunters had built of twigs and branches at the edge of the salt-lick when we heard the truck coming.

Hemingway); these letters and further notes written by Hemingway scholars are incredibly interesting in that they reveal more about the writer and his works than his stories and novels ever can.

...on stage and screen: Hemingway's bigger-than-life personality has been the topic of many movies, including *Papa Hemingway in Cuba* (2015) and *Genius* (2016) and as a character in *Midnight in Paris* (2011, written and directed by Woody Allen) who introduces the main character (played by Owen Wilson) to Gertrude Stein. The bar at the Ritz Hotel in Paris is named the Hemingway Bar.

In his book *The Critics and Hemingway, 1924-2014: Shaping an American Literary Icon*, Laurence Mazzeno writes that the first movie based on a Hemingway novel was shown in 1932, and, in 2013, a ballet version of *The Sun Also Rises* was performed at Washington, DC's Kennedy Center.[4]

...in comic books: Ernest Hemingway has even appeared in comics around the world. In one, be battles alongside Wolverine, fighting fascism in the Spanish Civil War (Wolverine traveled back in time).

...on social media: Hemingway has kept up with the times, with several Twitter and Facebook pages in his name. For example, readers can visit @DailyHemingway to enjoy quotations on a variety of subjects.

...in the White House: President Barack Obama listed *For Whom the Bell Tolls* as one of his favorite books, explaining that it "inspired" him.[5]

...throughout the world and beyond: There are many statues and plaques to Ernest Hemingway throughout the world and many places where you can walk where he walked. An outer planet was also named after him. Most

Each year crowds descend upon Key West to celebrate
Hemingway and his works at the Hemingway Days Festival. The
lookalike contest, seen here, is always a popular event.

important, though, is the mark Ernest Hemingway left on the art of writing.

His history of being a burly world traveler who would pay rough fishermen to box with him at his house in Key West is almost as well-known as his literature. It is his literature, though, that has influenced generations of writers after him. His writing style changed American literature just as Mark Twain's style changed it in his day. Ernest Hemingway was one of the most influential writers of the twentieth century, and readers can still learn much from his stories and books. Readers are given some clues in his writing, but they have to think about what they mean, and this is really the true joy in reading the literature of Ernest Hemingway.

CHRONOLOGY

1899– July 21: Ernest Miller Hemingway is born in Oak Park, Illinois.

1917– Graduates from Oak Park High School; moves to Kansas City to work as a reporter for the *Kansas City Star.*

1918– Begins service as an ambulance driver in Italy for the Red Cross.
July 8: Seriously wounded in Fossalta, Italy.

1919– Returns to Oak Park as a war hero.

1920– Moves to Chicago; finds work as a writer and editor.

1921– September 3: Marries first wife Hadley Richardson.
Leaves for Paris, France, to work as a foreign correspondent for the *Toronto Star.*

1923– *Three Stories and Ten Poems* and *in our time* are published.
October 10: Son, John Hadley Nicanor Hemingway ("Bumby") is born.

1925– *In Our Time* is published.

1926– *The Torrents of Spring* and *The Sun Also Rises* are published.
August: Legally separated from Hadley.

1927– May 10: Marries second wife Pauline Pfeiffer.

1928– June 28: Son Patrick Hemingway is born.
December 6: Father, Clarence, commits suicide.

1929– *A Farewell to Arms* is published.

1931– Moves to Key West, Florida.
November 12: Son Gregory Hancock Hemingway is born.

1932– *Death in the Afternoon* is published.

1933– *Winner Take Nothing* is published.

1935– *Green Hills of Africa* is published.

1937— *To Have and Have Not* is published.
Covers Spanish Civil War as correspondent.

1938— Publishes the play, *The Fifth Column*.

1939— Legally separated from Pauline.

1940— *For Whom the Bell Tolls* is published.
November 21: Marries third wife, Martha Gellhorn.

1941— Goes to China to cover the Chinese-Japanese War.

1942— Patrols Cuban waters, searches for German U-boats.

1944— Works as war correspondent in Europe; witnesses D-Day landing on Omaha Beach.

1945— Divorced from Martha.

1946— March 14: Marries fourth wife, Mary Welsh.

1950— *Across the River and into the Trees* is published.

1951— June 28: Mother, Grace, dies.

1952— *The Old Man and the Sea* is published after being serialized in *Life* magazine.

1953— Awarded Pulitzer Prize for *The Old Man and the Sea*.

1954— Suffers injuries in two separate plane crashes.
Awarded Nobel Prize in Literature.

1960— Leaves Cuba because of political changes; moves to Idaho.

1961— July 1: Commits suicide in Ketchum, Idaho.

1964— *A Moveable Feast* is published.

1965— The Hemingway Foundation is established.

1970— *Islands in the Stream* is published.

1980— The Hemingway Society is founded.

1985— *The Dangerous Summer* is published.

1986— *The Garden of Eden* is published.

1999— *True at First Light* is published.

2005— *Under Kilimanjaro* is published.

2011— *The Letters of Ernest Hemingway* project begins. First volume (of a probable seventeen) is published.

2015— *Ernest Hemingway: The Last Interview and Other Conversations* is published.

CHAPTER NOTES

Chapter 1. "The Dignity of Movement of an Iceberg": The Times and Places of Ernest Hemingway

1. Ernest Hemingway, *Death in the Afternoon* (New York: Scribner's, 1932), p. 192.
2. Ernest Hemingway, in *The Complete Short Stories* (New York: Quality Paperback Book Club, 1993), p. 288.
3. Ibid., p. 206.
4. Ernest Hemingway, *A Moveable Feast* (New York: Scribner's, 1964), p. 29.
5. Ernest Hemingway, *By-Line*, ed. William White (New York: Simon & Schuster, 1998), p. 219.
6. Ernest Hemingway, *The Sun Also Rises* (New York: Quality Paperback Book Club, 1993), p. 114.
7. Ernest Hemingway, *A Farewell to Arms* (New York: Quality Paperback Book Club, 1993), p. 185.
8. Ernest Hemingway, *In Our Time* (New York: Scribner's, 1958), p. 177.
9. Ibid, p. 179.

Chapter 2. From Oak Park to Paris and Beyond: The Making of the Writer

1. Carlos Baker, *Ernest Hemingway: The Writer as Artist* (Princeton, NJ: Princeton University Press, 1990), p. 5. Also in James R. Mellow, *Hemingway: A Life Without Consequences* (New York: Houghton Mifflin, 1992), p. 6.
2. Pam Johnson, "Making Values Visible," *Poynter Online*, November 11, 2002, http://www.poynter.org/2002/making-values-visible/3219/.
3. Ernest Hemingway, "Night Before Battle," *The Complete Short Stories* (New York: Quality Paperback Book Club, 1993), p. 437.
4. Ernest Hemingway, *A Moveable Feast*, p. 12.
5. Ernest Hemingway, *Complete Poems*, ed. Nicholas Gerogiannis (Lincoln, NE: University of Nebraska Press, 1992), p. xxiii.

Chapter 3. The Modern Short Story Collection: *In Our Time*

1. Ernest Hemingway, *In Our Time* (New York: Scribner's, 1958), p. 175.
2. Ibid, p. 213.
3. James R. Mellow, *Hemingway: A Life Without Consequences* (New York: Houghton Mifflin), p. xx.
4. David Wyatt, *Hemingway, Style, and the Art of Emotion* (New York: Cambridge University Press), p. 14.
5. Ernest Hemingway, *For Whom the Bell Tolls*, p. 73.
6. Ibid, p. 169.
7. Ernest Hemingway, unpublished draft of *A Farewell to Arms* (Item #168, The Hemingway Collection, JFK Library, Boston.)
8. Ernest Hemingway *A Moveable Feast* (New York: Charles Scribner's Sons, 1964), p. 76.
9. Ernest Hemingway, *The Complete Short Stories* (New York: Quality Paperback Book Club, 1993), p. 168.
10. Ernest Hemingway, *A Farewell to Arms* (New York: Quality Paperback Book Club, 1993), p. 243.
11. Hemingway, *In Our Time*, p. 81.
12. Hemingway in *The Complete Short Stories*, p. 221.
13. Hemingway, *In Our Time*, p. 21.
14. Ibid.
15. Ibid, p. 211.

Chapter 4. The Great Cycle of Life: *The Sun Also Rises*: Bumming Around Europe

1. Ernest Hemingway, *In Our Time* (New York: Scribner's, 1958), pp. 146–147.
2. Ibid, p. 147.
3. Ibid, p. 212.
4. Ernest Hemingway, *The Complete Short Stories* (New York: Quality Paperback Book Club, 1993), p. 291.
5. Ibid.
6. Ernest Hemingway, *The Sun Also Rises* (New York: Quality Paperback Book Club, 1993), p. 11.
7. Ibid, p. 31.

8. Ibid, p. 55.

9. Ibid, p. 247.

Chapter 5. Love and Guns: "Francis Macomber" and *A Farewell to Arms*

1. Carlos Baker, *Ernest Hemingway: Selected Letters* (London: Granada, 1972), p. 176.

2. James R. Mellow, *Hemingway: A Life Without Consequences*, p. 379.

3. Ernest Hemingway, *A Farewell to Arms* (New York: Quality Paperback Book Club, 1993), p. 3.

4. Ibid, p. 4.

5. Ibid, p. 184.

6. Rena Sanderson, Sandra Spanier, and Robert W. Trogdon, eds., *The Letters of Ernest Hemingway* (New York: Cambridge University Press, 2011), p. 26.

7. "The Private Hemingway," *The New York Times*, Febrary 15, 1981.

8. Ernest Hemingway, "The Short, Happy Life of Francis Macomber," *The Complete Short Stories* (New York: Quality Paperback Book Club, 1993), p. 27.

9. Ibid, p. 6.

10. Ibid.

11. Ibid.

12. Ibid.

13. Ibid, p. 21.

14. Carlos Baker, *Ernest Hemingway: A Life Story* (New York: Scribner Book Company, 1999), p. 339.

15. John Donne, *Devotions Upon Emergent Occasions* (London: McGill-Queen's University Press, 1975), p. 87.

16. Ernest Hemingway, *For Whom the Bell Tolls* (New York: Quality Paperback Book Club, 1993), p. 41.

17. Ibid, p. 466

18. Ibid, p. 15.

19. David Wyatt, *Hemingway, Style, and the Art of Emotion* (New York: Cambridge University Press, 2015), p. 148.

20. Hemingway, *For Whom the Bell Tolls*, p. 267.

21. Wyatt, p. 166.

22. Baker, *Ernest Hemingway: A Life Story*, p. 363.

Chapter 6. "I Went Out Too Far": *The Old Man and the Sea*

1. Ernest Hemingway, *The Old Man and the Sea* (New York: Scribner, 1995), p. 14.

2. Ibid, p. 12.

3. Ernest Hemingway, *The Complete Short Stories* (New York: Quality Paperback Book Club, 1993).

4. Carlos Baker, *Ernest Hemingway: A Life Story* (New York: Scribner Book Company, 1999), p. 504.

5. Hemingway, *The Old Man and the Sea*, p. 103.

6. Ibid, p. 110.

7. Ibid, p. 29.

8. Ibid., p. 107.

Chapter 7. The Sun Sets: Life Takes Its Toll

1. Ernest Hemingway, "Ernest Hemingway— Banquet Speech," *Nobelprize.org*, n.d., http://www.nobelprize.org/nobel_prizes/literature/laureates/1954/hemingway-speech.html, accessed October 27, 2016.

2. Ernest Hemingway, *Green Hills of Africa* (New York: Scribners, 1935), p. 22.

Chapter 8. The Hemingway Legacy: Ernest Hemingway and his Work Today

1. Ernest Hemingway, *For Whom the Bell Tolls*, (New York: Quality Paperback Book Club, 1993), pp. 463–464.

2. Ernest Hemingway, *A Moveable Feast*, (New York: Scribner's, 1964), p. 12.

3. Ibid, p. 209.

4. Laurence Mazzeno, *The Critics and Hemingway, 1924-2014: Shaping an American Literary Icon* (Rochester, NY: Camden House, 2015), p. 2.

5. Martin Chilton, "President Barack Obama's Favourite Books," *Telegraph*, April 21, 2016.

LITERARY TERMS

allegory A writing device in which a person, object, or event has more than one meaning. The incident of Santiago and the marlin in *The Old Man and the Sea* could be an allegory of the life of Jesus Christ.

allusion A writing device in which a scene, person, or event in one book or story refers to a similar thing in another book or story. For example, parts of *The Old Man and the Sea* can be seen as allusions to *Moby Dick*.

code hero A type of Hemingway character who is confident in his beliefs and shows "grace under pressure."

irony The use of a word or words to express an idea that is opposite that of the word's literal meaning, and when the actual outcome of events is different from what was expected. In modernism, this often involves the idea of humans being rewarded and punished at random.

modernism In literature, an era when writers wanted to break from the style of the past to explore new ways of writing. The movement is a little different in Europe and America, but it could be said to span from 1900 to 1960. The era signaled a shift toward more realistic writing.

parody A work in which one writer imitates and exaggerates another writer's work.

realism Writing that emphasizes people and situations that are more true to everyday life.

romanticism A movement in writing that emphasizes passion and imagination over realism.

symbol Something that represents or suggests another person or thing.

theme A distinctive concern or idea that is prevalent in a work of fiction.

vignette A short piece of descriptive writing that shows one moment; a scene without a traditional ending.

Major Works by
Ernest Hemingway

Three Stories and Ten Poems (1923)
in our time (1923)
In Our Time (1925)
The Torrents of Spring (1926)
The Sun Also Rises (1926)
Men Without Women (1927)
A Farewell to Arms (1929)
Death in the Afternoon (1932)
Winner Take Nothing (1933)
Green Hills of Africa (1935)
To Have and Have Not (1937)
The Spanish Earth (1938)
The Fifth Column and the First Forty-Nine Stories (1938)
For Whom the Bell Tolls (1940)
Men at War [edited by Hemingway] (1942)
Across the River and into the Trees (1950)
The Old Man and the Sea (1952)
A Moveable Feast (1964)
By-Line: Ernest Hemingway (1967)
Islands in the Stream (1970)
The Nick Adams Stories (1972)
Complete Poems (1979)
The Garden of Eden (1986)
True at First Light (1999)

Further Reading

Baker, Carlos. *Ernest Hemingway: The Writer as Artist*. Princeton, NJ: Princeton University Press, 1990.

Hotchner, A.E. *Hemingway in Love: His Own Story*. New York: St. Martin's Press, 2015.

Josephs, Allen. *On Hemingway and Spain: Essays and Reviews, 1979-2013*. Wickford, RI: New Street Communications, 2014.

Reynolds, Michael. *Hemingway* (several biographical volumes: *The Young Hemingway, The Paris Years, The 1930's, The American Homecoming, The Final Years*). New York: W.W. Norton, 1989–2000.

Sanderson, Rena, Sandra Spanier, and Robert W. Trogdon, eds. *The Letters of Ernest Hemingway* (an estimated 17 volumes—in progress). New York: Cambridge University Press (Volume 1, 2011).

Wyatt, David. *Hemingway, Style, and the Art of Emotion*. New York: Cambridge University Press, 2015.

WEBSITES

The Comics Journal
www.tcj.com/when-wolverine-met-hemingway-a-history-of-ernest-hemingway-in-comics-part-i
Extensive listing of comics and graphic novels featuring Ernest Hemingway from 1950 to today.

The Ernest Hemingway Collection at the JFK Presidential Library and Museum
www.jfklibrary.org/Research/The-Ernest-Hemingway-Collection.aspx
The largest collection of Hemingway's letters and notes for his writing, including online photos and information.

The Ernest Hemingway Foundation of Oak Park
www.ehfop.org
Information on Hemingway's birthplace, with a video tour, photos, and a newsletter.

Hemingway Editor App
www.hemingwayapp.com
An app to help your writing sound like the master's (not free).

PBS American Masters: Ernest Hemingway
www.pbs.org/wnet/americanmasters/ernest-hemingway-reflections-on-ernest-hemingway/629
Facts and criticism on Hemingway and his life as well as a video.

Timeless Hemingway
www.timelesshemingway.com
A huge resource of biographical information and criticism. Lots of links.

INDEX

A

Across the River and Into the Trees,
   90–91
African safaris, 74– 77, 79, 74, 100
Agassiz Club, 26, 27
airplane crashes, 100, 102
alcohol, 17, 61, 103
allegory, 91, 98
allusion, 97, 98
Anderson, Sherwood, 65

B

"Babylon Revisited," 63–64
Bible, 11, 26, 60, 72, 98
"Big Two-Hearted River," 17, 18, 22,
   44, 47–48, 52, 58, 108
boxing, 29, 35, 37, 50, 114
bullfighting, 17, 37, 38, 40, 41, 44,
   59, 72, 74, 103
"Butterfly and the Tank, The," 93–94

C

Caporetto retreat, 27, 40
Cézanne, Paul, 11, 14, 35, 36
Christianity, 9, 26, 31, 59, 98
"Clean, Well-Lighted Place, A," 8,
   58–59, 90
codes/code heroes, 42, 43, 48, 74, 75,
   77, 79, 85, 94, 108
Collier's, 90
Conrad, Joseph, 14
Crane, Hart, 16
"Cross Country Snow," 55, 57, 63
crucifixion, 98
Cuba, 80, 88, 90, 91, 105, 110
Cummings, e.e., 16

D

Dark Laughter, 65
D-Day, 90
Death in the Afternoon, 7, 74
"Death of Ivan Ilyich, The, " 92

depression, 103, 105
Devotions Upon Emergent
   Occasions, 81
"Did You Ever Kill Anyone?," 43
dignity, 93, 94, 95, 97, 108
Donne, John, 81, 85
dos Passos, John, 16, 80

E

Ecclesiastes, 60
electroshock therapy, 104
euphony, 30

F

Farewell to Arms, A, 33, 46, 48, 67,
   68, 70–72, 108, 111
fascism, 16–17, 20, 80, 84, 86, 112
Faulkner, William, 94–95, 97
Federal Bureau of Investigation
   (FBI), 88, 90, 104
Finca Vigia, 80
fishing, 16, 17, 18, 24, 25, 33, 35, 47,
   52, 58, 65, 67, 79, 88, 91–92, 95,
   97, 98, 100, 110,   111
Fitzgerald, F. Scott, 16, 53, 61, 62,
   63, 65, 68
five senses, importance of to
   Hemingway's writing, 21, 46
For Whom the Bell Tolls, 45–46, 81,
   83– 87, 90, 108, 111, 112

G

Garden of Eden, The, 106
German submarines, Hemingway's
   hunt for, 88, 90
Green Hills of Africa, 74, 102, 111
Gris, Juan, 11

H

Heart of Darkness, 14
Hemingway, Clarence (father), 24,
   25, 26, 27, 29, 52, 68
Hemingway, Ernest

Hemingway, Elizabeth "Hadley" (wife), 33, 37, 38, 54, 59, 60, 65
Hemingway, Ernest
  as ambulance driver during World War I, 9, 31, 33, 68, 70, 80
  childhood, 24–27, 29
  children, 38, 65, 67, 74, 105
  comic book portrayals, 112
  death, 105, 108
  education, 13, 27, 29
  festivals in his honor, 110
  influences, 13–14
  injuries/illnesses, 31, 33, 37, 67, 70, 74, 100, 102, 103–105
  journalism career, 21–22, 23, 29–30, 33, 36, 37, 47, 80, 90, 100
  legacy, 106, 108–110, 112, 114
  marriages, 33, 37, 38, 54, 59, 60, 65, 67, 74, 80, 88, 90, 100, 102, 103, 104, 105
  origin of Papa nickname, 54
  parents, 24, 25, 26, 29, 52, 68
  portrayals in film, 112
  social media accounts concerning, 112
Hemingway, Grace (mother), 24, 25
Hemingway, Gregory (son), 74
Hemingway, John (son), 38, 65
Hemingway, Martha (wife), 80, 88, 90
Hemingway, Mary (wife), 88, 90, 100, 102, 103, 104, 105
Hemingway, Patrick (son), 67
Hemingway, Pauline (wife), 65, 67, 74, 80
Hemingway's Selected Letters 1917–1961, 106
Huckleberry Finn, 102
humor, 75
iceberg theory, 7, 8, 44, 49, 53, 70, 72, 110

"In Another Country," 13
"Indian Camp," 43–44, 52–53
In Our Time, 38, 39–42, 44, 47–48, 49, 52–53, 111
irony, 20, 41, 42, 97, 110
Islands in the Stream, 106
Italy, 9, 13, 31, 33, 48, 70, 75, 90
Ivens, Joris, 80

J
Jesus Christ, 98, 99
journalism, influence on Hemingway's style, 21–23, 30, 47

K
Kansas City Star, 21, 22, 29–30, 47, 100
Ketchum (Idaho), 103, 104, 105, 110
Key West, 65, 67, 74, 79, 110, 114
"Killers, The," 49–50, 52

L
Lardner, Ring, 14
"L'Envoi," 41
Life, 91
"Light of the World, The," 94
Lost Generation, 14, 16–17, 20, 21, 55, 60, 61, 63, 93, 110

M
malaria, 37
Melville, Herman, 99
Michigan, 25, 27, 33, 43
Miró, Joan, 14
Moby Dick, 97–98, 99
modernism, 9, 11, 18, 39
Moveable Feast, A, 47, 106, 109, 111

N
"Natural History of the Dead, A," 26–27
Nick Adams stories, 16, 17, 18, 22, 42–45, 47–48, 49–50, 52–53, 55, 57–58, 108

nicknames, 26, 54
nihilism, 58–59
Nobel Prize, 87, 102

O

Oak Park (Illinois), 24, 26, 29, 33, 110
Obama, Barack, 112
Old Man and the Sea, The, 91–93, 93, 94–95, 97–99, 100, 111
"Old Man at the Bridge," 94
one true sentence, examples of, 111
open endings, 39

P

Paris, 17, 33, 35, 42, 53, 55, 62, 63, 67, 80, 109, 110
parody, 65
Peele, George, 70
Perkins, Max, 70
Picasso, Pablo, 14, 53
Pilar, 79, 88
pity, 20, 95, 97, 110
poetry, 11, 17, 35, 36, 37, 38, 53, 81, 102
Pound, Ezra, 35
profanity/profane subject matter, 70, 87
Pulitzer Prize, 100

R

realism, 9, 12, 13
Red Cross, 31, 68, 70
Renaissance man, explanation of, 35
romanticism, 9, 12

S

separate peace, 48–49
Shakespeare, William, 11, 27, 60
"Short Happy Life of Francis Macomber, The," 74–77, 79
Spain, 37, 38, 59–60, 80, 81, 83–87, 103
Spanish Civil War, 16, 24, 80, 81, 83–87, 88, 112

Spanish Earth, The, 80
Stein, Gertrude, 14, 18, 35, 37, 48, 53, 60, 112
suicide, 52, 68, 105
Sun Also Rises, The, 16, 18, 20, 38, 55, 60–65, 95, 111

T

telegrams, 23
Tender Is the Night, 61
Three Stories and Ten Poems, 37
Tolstoy, Leo, 92
Toronto, 33, 38
Toronto Star Weekly, 33, 36
Torrents of Spring, The, 65
True at First Light, 106
Twain, Mark, 102, 114

V

Victorian era, 9
vignette, 39
visual arts, 11, 12–13, 14, 35, 36
von Kurowsky, Agnes, 33

W

Walloon Lake, 25
World War I, 16, 17, 29, 31, 43, 47, 48, 61, 68, 70, 80
World War II, 16, 88, 90